# A Woman's Place is in the Cabinet

Women ministers in governments of the

Republic of Ireland 1919-2019

## Maedhbh McNamara

### Sea Dog Books

First Published in Ireland by Sea Dog Books, in 2020, and produced in co-operation with Choice Publishing, Drogheda, County Louth, Republic of Ireland.
www.choicepublishing.ie

Paperback ISBN: 978-1-913275-06-8
eBook ISBN: 978-1-913275-07-5

A CIP catalogue record for this book is available from the National Library.

**Cover Design:** Johanna Lowry O'Reilly

## Front cover photo

Group of 4 former Tánaistí (deputy prime ministers) at the Royal Irish Academy in 2018
Left to right: Mary Harney, Joan Burton, Mary Coughlan and Frances Fitzgerald.

**Photograph:** Dave Meehan

## Back cover photo

Photo: Group of 14 current and former government ministers at Lissadell in Sligo in July 2018, to commemorate Constance Markievicz, the first female Minister (with Constance Cassidy, centre).

**Front row** (left to right): Frances Fitzgerald, Gemma Hussey, Constance Cassidy, Máire Geoghegan-Quinn, Mary O'Rourke, Katherine Zappone.

**Back row** (left to right): Niamh Bhreathnach, Jan O'Sullivan, Nora Owen, Mary Harney, Mary Mitchell O'Connor, Mary Coughlan, Mary Hanafin, Síle de Valera, Heather Humphries.

Not present on the day: Joan Burton, Regina Doherty, Josepha Madigan
Deceased: Constance Markievicz, Eileen Desmond

**Photograph:** James Connolly

# Contents

## 8 Mary Harney 34
Tánaiste. Progressive Democrats. (until 2009).
26 June 1997- 13 September 2006 28th Dáil, 29th Dáil.
Minister for Enterprise, Trade and Employment. 26 June 1997-
13 September 2004. 28th Dáil, 29th Dáil
Minister for Health and Children. 29 September 2004 - 19 January 2011.
29th Dáil 30th Dáil. Independent (2009–2011)

## 9 Síle de Valera 45
Minister for Arts, Heritage, Gaeltacht and the Islands.
Fianna Fáil. 26 June 1997 - 6 June 2002. 28th Dáil

## 10 Mary Coughlan 50
Minister for Social and Family Affairs. Fianna Fáil.
17 June 2002- 29 September 2004. 29th Dáil
Minister for Agriculture, Fisheries and Food 29 September 2004 -
7 May 2008. 29th Dáil. 30th Dáil
Tánaiste . 7 May 2008 - 9 March 2011. 30th Dáil
Minister for Enterprise, Trade and Employment.
7 May 2008 - 23 March 2010.
Minister for Education and Skills. 23 March 2010- 9 March 2011
Minister for Health and Children. 20 January 2011- 9 March 2011

## 11 Mary Hanafin 55
Minister for Education and Science. Fianna Fáil.
29 September 2004 - 7 May 2008 29th Dáil, 30th Dáil.
Minister for Social and Family Affairs. 7 May 2008 - 23 March 2010.
30th Dáil. Minister for Tourism, Culture and Sport.
23 March 2010- 9 March 2011.
Minister for Enterprise, Trade and Innovation.
20 January 2011- 9 March 2011

## 12 Joan Burton 60
Minister for Social Protection. Labour.
9 March 2011- 6 May 2016. 31st Dáil Tánaiste.
4 July 2014- 6 May 2016.

**Glossary**

Taoiseach: Prime Minister
Tánaiste: Deputy Prime Minister
Uachtarán: President
Áras an Uachtaráin: President's House
Oireachtas, Houses of the: parliament
Ceann Comhairle: Speaker of parliament
Dáil Éireann: lower house of parliament
Seanad Éireann: upper house of parliament
Gaeltacht: Irish-speaking areas
TD: Teachta Dála (Member of Parliament)
FG: Fine Gael political party
FF: Fianna Fáil political party
Lab: Labour Party
SF: Sinn Féin

# Foreword

## by Joan Burton TD, Tánaiste July 2014-May 2016

Experts often say that politics is a numbers game.

Every time a new Cabinet is appointed we get the traditional "family photograph" of the President and the Ministers holding their precious seals of office at Áras an Uachtaráin.

So, let me take you on a tour of an imaginary wall in a Leinster House corridor that features all these solemn photos from the First Dáil in January 1919 to the present day. Constance Markievicz served as Minister for Labour in the pre-independence Government 1919 to 1922 but from then all through those decades to Mr Haughey's first Fianna Fáil Government in December 1979 there is not a single female face. Yes, none. Zero women.

That particular photo of the 1979-1982 Government shows Máire Geoghegan-Quinn on the day of her appointment as Minister for the Gaeltacht, a genuinely revolutionary moment. Every Cabinet after that had at least one woman Minister but even today we are way off any gender equality around the Cabinet Table.

When I became Tánaiste in July 2014, I told Taoiseach Enda Kenny I proposed to have 2 women among Labour's 5 Ministers and urged him to add more to his team. He did add 1 more so that Cabinet had 5 women around the table including Máire Whelan* as Attorney General. Today there are only 4.

While all Cabinet Ministers are constitutionally equal everyone knows that some positions are more equal than others.

The posts of Taoiseach along with Finance, Foreign Affairs and Justice are the great offices of State and command particular influence in any

Cabinet. Traditionally women Ministers are pigeon-holed into social departments such as Education, Health or Social Welfare.

To date no woman has held office as Taoiseach or Minister for Finance or Foreign Affairs. Finance, of course, has massive power and has been held steadfastly in male hands in the whole history of the State and indeed the main roles associated with that Department, Secretary Generals and Governor of the Central Bank have all been held by men.

Máire Geoghegan-Quinn broke another glass ceiling by becoming the first female Minister for Justice in the FF-Labour Cabinet in 1993. In that role she displayed special skill in piloting the repeal of antiquated anti-gay laws that Labour had demanded.

Numbers do matter. As I write this** the heads of EU Governments are discussing the share out of the leading posts in the Commission, Parliament, Central Bank and Council of Ministers. Reports suggest that at least 2 of the main roles will go to women.

Gender equality in high political office is firmly on the international agenda. It cannot come too soon.

I welcome this addition to Irish political history.

Joan Burton TD represents Dublin West in Dáil Éireann. She served as Minister of State 1993-1997 and later as Minister for Social Protection 2011-2016 and Tánaiste 2014-2016.

*Máire Whelan was the first woman Attorney General (2011-2017) in Ireland. Attorneys General in their capacity as legal adviser to the Government attend Government meetings.

**In May 2019. Two such roles went to Ursula Von der Leyen, President of the European Commission and Christine Lagarde, nominated as President of the European Central Bank.

# Introduction

Between 1919 and 2019, 19 women have served as cabinet ministers in governments of Ireland. Just 10 per cent of those who have held senior ministerial positions in that 100 years have been women, totalling 19 women politicians.

These ministers served in the Republic of Ireland and its predecessors the Irish Free State (1922–1937) and the Irish Republic (1919–1922).

The appointment of Constance Markievicz as Minister for Labour in the First Dáil in 1919 seemed a promising beginning for women in government. But in 1921, when the Dáil Cabinet was reorganised, Labour was no longer a full Cabinet post and Markievicz was left out of the inner circle of Ministers.

Mary MacSwiney, a contemporary TD, expressed a hope that this was not setting a precedent. Her concern was prophetic.

60 years after the first woman Minister was appointed to Cabinet, the second, Máire Geoghegan Quinn, was appointed Minister for the Gaeltacht in 1979.

After the gap of more than a half-century between the first and second women ministers, and another lacuna in the government of the 23rd Dáil, there has been at least one woman in all Cabinets since December 1982.

Women have also served as junior ministers outside Cabinet. (Junior ministers were termed Parliamentary Secretaries until 1978, and since then have been known as Ministers of State.[1])

---

[1] Biographical notes about all elected women deputies and senators, including junior ministers, are found in McNamara, Maedhbh and Paschal Mooney. *Women in Parliament Ireland: 1918-2000 with updated directory of women in Dáil, Seanad and Presidency 1918-2018,* Sea Dog Books, 2020, from which this book is extracted.

See also McNamara, Maedhbh and Paschal Mooney. Women in parliament 1918-2000. Dublin, Wolfhound, 2000.

Four women have reached the high office of Tánaiste (deputy prime minister).

The first was Mary Harney, leader of the Progressive Democrat party and longest-serving woman minister in the history of the State. The second was Mary Coughlan, deputy leader of Fianna Fáil. Then came Joan Burton, leader of the Labour Party. Fourth was Frances Fitzgerald of the Fine Gael party.

*Tánaistí (left to right): Mary Harney (Progressive Democrats), Joan Burton (Labour Party), Mary Coughlan (Fianna Fáil) and Frances Fitzgerald (Fine Gael) at a Royal Irish Academy Discourse in 2018.*

*Photo: Dave Meehan*

No woman has ever been Taoiseach (Prime Minister). No woman has yet been appointed Minister for Finance or Minister for Defence or Minister for Foreign Affairs. These are the last male ministerial redoubts in Irish cabinet life.

The Constitution provides for governments of 15 ministers upwards. No more than four women have served simultaneously in any Cabinet.

The 31st Government of Ireland, formed in June 2017, included four (26.6%) women ministers out of a total of 15 ministers in the Cabinet: Heather Humphreys (Business), Katherine Zappone (Children), Regina Doherty (Social Protection) and Josepha Madigan (Arts, Heritage and

Gaeltacht). This represents the highest proportion of women in Irish senior ministerial positions, the previous highest being four (26.6%) in 2011, and three (20%) in 2007 and in 1997.

There are also three woman Ministers of State out of a total of 19 in the 31st government.

While Ireland has not yet had a woman Prime Minister, it has elected two distinguished women Presidents, Mary Robinson and Mary McAleese.

The women ministers have been high achievers in politics. They are trailblazers and, for the most part, have left a substantial legislative legacy.

They fought the same battles as men and made a considerable contribution to Irish life.

This book addresses the contributions they have made.

# Constance Markievicz, née Gore-Booth

Date/Place of birth: 4 February 1868/Buckingham Gate, London
Party: Sinn Féin. Fianna Fáil, 1926-1927 (death)
Constituency: Dublin St. Patrick's/Dublin Borough South
Dáil/ Seanad: 1st, 2nd Dáil (14 December 1918-15 June 1922),
4th, 15th Dáil (27 August 1923-5 July 1927 (death))
Age at entry to Dáil: 50
Family: Married Count Casimir Dunin-Markievicz. One daughter.
Grand-daughter of Sir Robert Gore-Booth, M.P. for County Sligo 1850-1876.

Education: Governess at home. Slade School, London; Rodolphe Julian Art School, Paris.
Occupation: Artist and revolutionary
Date of Death: 15 July 1927
Address: 1 Ballinvoher, Drumcliffe East, Sligo (1911 census).1 Frankfort Avenue, Rathgar; Frankfort House, Rathgar (last address)
Publications: *James Connolly's Policy and Catholic Doctrine*, 1924. What Irish republicans stand for. Glasgow, Civic Press, 1922. Broken dreams: a three-act play. Eva Gore-Booth and Esther Roper. *Prison Letters of Countess Markievicz.* London: Virago, 1987 (reissue, with new introduction, of 1934 Longmans Green edition). Naughton, Lindie (editor). Markievicz: prison letters & rebel writings. Newbridge, Merrion Press, 2018.
Naughton, Lindie. Markievicz: a most outrageous rebel. Newbridge, Merrion, 2016. Haverty, Anne. Markievicz: an independent Life. London, Pandora, 1993. Marreco, Anne. The rebel countess: the life and times of Constance Markievicz. London, Phoenix Press, 1967. McGowan, Joe (editor). Constance Markievicz: the people's countess. Sligo, Markievicz Millennium Committee, 2003. Norman, Diana. Terrible beauty: a life of Constance Markievicz, 1868-1927. Swords, Poolbeg, 1987. Van Voris, Jacqueline. Constance de Markievicz in the cause of Ireland. Amherst, University of Massachusetts Press, 1967.

## Career:

Minister for Labour, 2 April 1919 - 9 January 1922. First Chair, Fianna Fáil. Founder Member, United Arts Club, 1907. Member, President, Theatre of Ireland company. Member, Inghinidhe na hÉireann, 1908. Member, Sinn Fein, 1908 —; its executive, 1909. Founder, Fianna na hÉireann, 1909.Member, Irish Citizen Army, 1913. Member, President, Cumann na mBan, 1914. Honorary president, Irish Women Workers' Union, 1917. Founder, Sligo branch of the Irish Women's Suffrage and Local Government Association, 1896.

**Constance Gore-Booth** was the daughter of Sir Henry Gore-Booth and his wife Georgina Hill, and grand-daughter of Sir Robert Gore-Booth MP and Colonel Hill of Tickhill Castle, Yorkshire. Her birth took place in London, where the family resided with Sir Robert Gore-Booth while the House of Commons was in session. Eva Gore-Booth, poet, suffragette and labour activist, was her sister. The family was descended from Sir Paul Gore, a soldier of fortune who established himself in Ireland in 1597 and from whom was also descended the family of Al Gore, the American Vice-President. During the 1750s there were nine Gores, almost certainly all cousins, in the Irish parliament, according to Sir Josslyn Gore-Booth. (See Dodd, John, 'Gore blimey', *The Spectator,* 22 January 2000). Christopher Hill, a relative of theirs, was a founding member of the Communist Party of Great Britain in 1920.

Constance was educated privately at Lissadell House, the landed estate in County Sligo where the three Gore-Booth generations lived together. Here W.B. Yeats set his poem, *'In Memory of Eva Gore-Booth and Con Markiewicz'.* She was presented at court to Queen Victoria in 1887. She studied art at the Slade School in London in 1893 and later in Paris (1898-1900).

In 1896 Constance and Eva with their sister Mabel established the first Sligo branch of the Irish Women's Suffrage and Local Government Association. For this they were derided by *Vanity Fair* magazine:

> .....*the three pretty daughters of Sir Henry Gore-Booth are creating a little excitement (not to say amusement) for the emancipation of their sex. Miss ... Gore-Booth and her sisters, supported by a few devoted yokels, have been holding a few meetings in connection with the Woman's Suffrage (or, shall I say, 'The Revolt of the Daughters?') movement.... The sisters make a pretty picture on the platform; but it is not women of their type who need to assert themselves over Man&Co.*

*However, it amuses them – ...and I doubt if the tyrant has much to fear from their little arrows.'*

('Vanity Fair,' London, 31st December 1896)

Constance allied the suffrage cause with that of the Drumcliffe Cooperative Society.

On 29 September 1900 in London Constance married Count Casimir Dunin-Markievicz, son of a Polish landowner in the Ukraine. Their only child, Maeve, was born in November, 1901 and the Markieviczs settled in Dublin in 1903.

With her husband and Ellen Duncan, Markievicz was a founder member of the United Arts Club in 1907. Through her interest in the Abbey Theatre and the Gaelic League, Constance found back numbers of the *Peasant* and *Sinn Féin* journals which sparked her interest in the nationalist movement. She entered Sinn Fein politics in 1908. She joined Inghinidhe na hEireann, a feminist society founded by Maud Gonne. At the first meeting of Inghinidhe na hÉireann, she took a diamond clip from her hair and laid it on the table for the funds. She wrote for its journal, *Bean na hÉireann*.

She and Eva supported the 'Manchester Barmaids', who were refused the right to work after 6pm and thus were unable to feed their families. A by-election was held in 1908, in which candidate Winston Churchill asserted that women were not entitled to work. Constance and Eva followed Churchill through the Manchester streets in a carriage drawn by four white horses whose heads were festooned in black feathers. Constance steered in the wake of Churchill's plain entourage and became a *cause célèbre*. It was reputed that a man heckled her: 'Can you cook a dinner, Madame?' to which she replied, 'Can you handle a coach and four?'

In 1909 she founded Na Fianna Éireann, an organisation for boys, to whom she taught drilling and the use of arms. Patrick Pearse said that without Na Fianna, there would have been no Volunteers in 1913, and the 1916 Easter Rising would have been impossible. Markievicz met the Irish labour leaders, James Connolly and James Larkin. She helped the workers in the 1913 Lockout of Dublin by running a soup kitchen in Liberty Hall, and joined the Citizen Army, led by Connolly.

In a lecture to the Irish Women's Franchise League in 1915 she recommended that women

> 'dress suitably in short skirts and strong boots, leave your jewels in the bank and buy a revolver... take your responsibilities and be prepared to go your own way depending for safety on your own courage, your own truth and your own common sense'.

During the 1916 Easter Rising Markievicz served with an Irish Citizen Army company as second-in-command to Commandant Mallin, in Saint Stephen's Green, under fire from British troops in the Shelbourne Hotel, Dublin. The Royal College of Surgeons had been closed for the duration, but one member of staff reported for work. The porter opened the door a chink to explain the situation. Markievicz and company seized the chance to commandeer the College and established their garrison in the Board Room. After laying down arms, she was court-martialled in Kilmainham Gaol, and sentenced to death. She was reprieved, however, and her sentence was commuted to penal servitude for life in Aylesbury Gaol. Released in the general amnesty of June 1917, the Countess converted to Catholicism and was made honorary president of the Irish Women Workers' Union. Sligo declared her a Freeman in August 1917.

She was re-arrested in May 1918. She contested the December 1918 general election from Holloway prison, and was elected to a seat in the Dublin constituency of St Patrick's. She was the first woman elected to the United Kingdom parliament, the only woman elected of 17 women candidates in the UK.

In a letter to Markievicz dated 5 February, 1919, the Prime Minister wrote:

Sir,

On Tuesday, February 11th, His Majesty will open parliament in person….I hope you may find it convenient to be in your place.

Yours faithfully, D. Lloyd George.

The envelope, addressed to *Madame Markievicz M.P., (St. Patrick's), Dublin*, has, in a different hand, the forwarding address of Holloway Gaol, London. [National Museum of Ireland HE-EW-875-G].

In accordance with Sinn Féin policy, she did not take her seat in Westminster. (Later, she visited the Members' vestibule to look at the peg reserved for her hat and coat.)

The Sinn Féin MPs elected to Westminster set up their own assembly and called it Dáil Éireann. Markievicz was a member of the first Dáil Eireann which met on 21 January 1919, and was released from Holloway prison on 10 March. She was appointed Minister for Labour on 2 April 1919, thereby becoming the first woman cabinet minister in Western Europe.

*When Madame Markievicz was made Minister for Labour she came rushing home to tell me. I asked her how she managed it, as I had noticed that the present leaders were not over-eager to put women into places of honour or power, even though they had earned the right to both, as well as the men had, having responded to every call made upon them throughout the struggle for freedom. She told me she had to bully them; she claimed she had earned the right to be a Minister as well as any of the men, and was equally as well fitted for it, educationally and every other way, and if she was not made a Minister she would go over to the Labour Party.*

(Clarke, Kathleen. Revolutionary woman: Kathleen Clarke 1878-1972: an autobiography. Edited by Helen Litton. Dublin, O'Brien Press, 1991)

Markievicz's first Dáil assignment was as a member of a committee appointed to consider prisoners of war and kidnapped children. This inquiry obtained their release, and the committee reported the return home of the kidnapped children. She was proscribed as a member of illegal organisations, served a prison sentence in Cork in 1919 and was also on the run. However, she continued work in her Labour ministry, where social welfare was also part of her remit. Her department was concerned with setting up Conciliation Boards, arbitrating labour disputes, surveying areas and establishing guidelines for wages and food prices.

While imprisoned in Mountjoy from January to July 1921 she was returned unopposed with all other nominees to the Second Dáil on 19 May 1921. She was re-appointed Minister for Labour on 26 August 1921. When the Dáil Cabinet was re-organised in 1921, Markievicz was left out of the inner circle of Ministers, as Labour was no longer a full Cabinet post. Mary MacSwiney TD (May 1921-June 1927) expressed concern, prophetically, that she hoped that this was not setting a precedent.

Markievicz served as Minister until 9 January, 1922. The Ministry's activities now included agricultural disputes involving the harvest bonus on several farms, and disputes in factories, offices and stores. Even where the authority of the Dáil was not recognised officially, cases were arbitrated by the Republican boards. Markievicz reported in December 1921 that on 15 September Tyrone County Council had submitted to the arbitration of her Labour Ministry a dispute between itself and the quarry workers it employed. Tyrone County Council functioned under the British Local Government Board, not the Dáil Éireann Local Government Department.

When arbitration failed, she threatened to use military force against religious bigotry, telling a Catholic quarry manager in the north that unless intimidation against a Protestant workman ceased, the matter would be put into the hands of the republican police. During intractable negotiations in one employment dispute, it was claimed that she pulled out her gun and told the employer "I give you ten minutes to settle, or I shoot" and that he settled in 7 minutes.

She proved effective in the role of Minister for Labour (Sonia Paseta. Vótáil 100 Conference, 'Representation, Gender and Politics: Past and Present', Royal Irish Academy, 1 February 2018).

Markievicz opposed the Anglo-Irish Treaty of 1921 and toured America in April and May 1922 to enlist support for the republican cause. She was defeated in the 1922 general election, then won a seat in Dublin Borough South in the August 1923 election when the Civil War had ended. In accordance with Sinn Féin policy she abstained from taking her seat. She was briefly on hunger strike after her arrest for advocating republicanism in November 1923.

She joined Fianna Fáil when it was founded by De Valera in 1926, and left Sinn Féin which had divided after the IRA had split from it. She also resigned from Cumann na mBan women's army, thereby abandoning violence and embracing parliamentary democracy.

Having been re-elected to the Dáil in 1927, she died in a public ward of Sir Patrick Dun's Hospital, in Dublin, on 15 July, 1927, surrounded by Casimir, family and friends. She was accorded a public funeral, for which the working class people lined the streets, and was buried at Glasnevin cemetery.

Constance Markievicz was shortlisted as a Woman of the Millennium by UK *Guardian* readers *(The Guardian,* 25 January 1999).

# Máire Geoghegan-Quinn

Date/Place of birth: 5 September 1950/Carna, County Galway
Party: Fianna Fáil
Constituency: Galway West
DÁIL/SEANAD: 20TH-27TH DÁIL (4 MARCH 1975-5 JUNE 1997).
EU COURT OF AUDITORS: MARCH 2000-FEBRUARY 2010
European Commission: Nominated in November 2009 for term in
office February 2010 to November 2014.
AGE AT ENTRY TO DÁIL: 24
FAMILY: DAUGHTER OF JOHN GEOGHEGAN (TD, GALWAY WEST 1954-75).
MARRIED TO JOHN V. QUINN; TWO SONS
EDUCATION: COLAISTE MHUIRE, TUAR MHIC EADAIGH, COUNTY MAYO, CARYSFORT TEACHERS' TRAINING COLLEGE,
BLACKROCK, COUNTY DUBLIN
OCCUPATION: PRIMARY SCHOOLTEACHER
PUBLICATIONS; *The Green Diamond* (a novel), Marino, 1996.
ADDRESS; CAPPAGH, BARNA, GALWAY

## Career:

Minister for Justice, 4 January 1993 – 15 December 1994 (first woman Minister for Justice). Minister for Equality and Law Reform, 18 November 1994-15 December 1994 (government changed without dissolution of Dáil). Minister for Tourism, Transport & Communications, February 1992-January 1993; Minister of State at the Department of the Taoiseach with special responsibility as co-ordinator of Government Policy and EC matters, March 1987-November 1991; Minister of State at the Department of Education with special responsibility for Youth & Sport, March-December 1982. Minister for the Gaeltacht, 1979-1981. Parliamentary Secretary to the Minister for Industry, Commerce & Energy, 1977-18, Minister of State at the Department 1978-9, with special responsibility for Consumer Affairs. Chairperson, first Joint Committee on Women's Rights, 1983-. Member, Joint Committee on Marriage Breakdown, 1983. Member, Special Committee on the Judicial Separation and Family Law Reform Bill, 1987, Member, Select Committee on Social Affairs, 10 March 1995. Member of Galway City Council 1985; Member of Galway Cheshire Home Committee; Chair, Wanting Older Women Well; Chair, Saffron Initiative; Chair of Fianna Fail. Columnist *The Irish Times,* 1997; Consultant to several companies; non-executive director, the Ryan Hotel Group; TV broadcaster.

**Maire Geoghegan-Quinn** was elected to the Dáil in March 1975, in a by-election in Galway West caused by the death of her father. She was the first woman in the State appointed to Cabinet when she was appointed Minister for the Gaeltacht in 1979. In opposition, she was Chair of the first parliamentary committee on women's rights in the 1980s. Geoghegan-Quinn became Ireland's first woman EU Commissioner.

On social issues she was on the liberal wing of Fianna Fáil, and supported, for example, family planning (birth control).

In an appearance before the Seanad in 2013 Geoghegan-Quinn recalled her early career:

*"...I remember the first time I came here, with a Consumer Information Bill, as long ago as 1977 or 1978. I learned more during the discussion in this chamber about the law and how it works than I could ever have learned in the Dáil.... The debate in the Dáil was fast and furious and there were so many items on the agenda. When I came into the Seanad there was a possibility to tease out the legislation. I did something I believe few of my predecessors had done - I accepted amendments. I may not have been very popular with my colleagues in the Dáil at the time but I believe it was a good thing to do."*

(Seanad Éireann. Address to Seanad Éireann by Commissioner Máire Geoghegan-Quinn, 8 May 2013).

In November 1991 she resigned her post of Minister of State at the Department of the Taoiseach in opposition to CJ Haughey's leadership. When Albert Reynolds succeeded Haughey the following year he appointed her Minister for Tourism, Transport and Communications. Upon informing the Dáil in 1992 of her request for proposals from the Aer Lingus board to solve the company's financial difficulties, she was accused by an opposition TD of hand-bagging the board. Hand-bagging was a term coined in relation to UK Prime Minister Thatcher which had become a colloquialism for women's assertiveness. Geoghegan-Quinn in the Chamber decried the sexism of this term and the expression was promptly deemed un-parliamentary.

She was a member of the team which negotiated the Joint Declaration on Peace and Reconciliation in Ireland of December 1993 by the British and Irish Governments.

In January 1993 she became Minister for Justice, in which office she undertook substantial law reform legislation, notably in the *Criminal Law (Sexual Offences) Act, 1993,* which decriminalised homosexual acts.

In December 1994, in the collapse of the Fianna Fáil/Labour government she lost office.

After the resignation of Reynolds as party leader, she announced that she would challenge Bertie Ahern for the leadership, but withdrew on the day of the planned ballot. Ahern appointed her to his new front bench.

Geoghegan-Quinn in 1996 published a novel *The Green Diamond,* whose protagonist is the student-teacher daughter of a Galway politician who wants her mother to become the first woman Taoiseach.

On 25 January 1997, Geoghegan-Quinn informed the Taoiseach of her decision to step down from politics, citing media intrusion into her family. Tribute was paid by journalist Vincent Browne:

> *Máire Geoghegan-Quinn is a huge loss to Irish politics. She is perhaps the finest public representative in Dáil Éireann. She has courage, clarity of expression, a fine intellect, integrity and decisiveness. She may be the greatest Taoiseach we never had.*
> (Irish Times, 29 January 1997).

On 29 July 1999, Geoghegan-Quinn was nominated by Taoiseach Ahern to the EU Court of Auditors, the body responsible for auditing the legality of EU spending and sound financial management, which highlights inefficiency and waste. From March 2000 to February 2010, she represented Ireland at the Court of Auditors in Luxemburg. She was in charge of auditing the EU's external action budget in areas such as overseas development aid. Her second 6-year term commenced in March 2006.

In 2009 a new European Commission was due. Commission President Barroso wrote to all EU prime ministers including Taoiseach Cowen, suggesting that they nominate a woman to the Commission in order to improve its gender balance. Nominating a woman could improve Ireland's chance of receiving a stronger Commission portfolio. Also, the government had a small majority in the Dáil and could ill afford to lose a TD. Geoghegan-Quinn was nominated in November 2009 for her term in office from February 2010 to November 2014.

She was allocated the Research and Innovation portfolio targeted by the Government. This was a mid-level mandate centred on restoring growth to the European economy through innovation. Her brief had a research budget of €58 billion and covered a range of bodies to encourage innovation, especially among Small and Medium Enterprises. They included the Joint Research Centre, European Research Council and Research Executive Agency, one of the world's biggest scientific research centres. She secured a budget increase to €80 billion (EU 2013. Irish Times, 10 January 2013). She was in charge of almost a quarter of the Commission staff.

Against Fine Gael Government policy, Geoghegan-Quinn declared that she would vote against the abolition of the Seanad in the 2013 referendum. Although EU Commissioners typically stay out of domestic political debate, Geoghegan-Quinn made the case for retention of the Seanad during a debate on her work in Brussels. (The electorate voted to retain the Seanad.)

As outgoing EU Commissioner, Geoghegan-Quinn was awarded Chevalier de la Légion d'Honneur, the highest honour bestowed by the French government. The award was a tribute to her "remarkable contribution to the European project", which included setting up Horizon 2020, the €80 billion EU programme for science, research and innovation.

*"This programme will be a central driver for the economic recovery process in Europe as it will create both high-skilled jobs and new goods and services,"* said the French secretary of state. She noted that the Irish commissioner had won the support of the 28 EU governments for the Horizon 2020 programme *"at a time of tight budgetary constraint"* (Irish Times, 25 September 2014).

# Eileen Desmond, née Harrington

DATE/PLACE OF BIRTH: 29 DECEMBER 1932/OLD HEAD, KINSALE, COUNTY CORK
PARTY: LABOUR
CONSTITUENCY: MID-CORK, CORK SOUTH CENTRAL.
SEANAD: INDUSTRIAL AND COMMERCIAL PANEL
DÁIL/SEANAD: 17TH DÁIL (10 MARCH 1965 (BY-ELECTION)-18 MARCH 1965),
18TH DÁIL (7 APRIL 1965-17 JUNE 1969). 20TH, 21ST, 22ND, 23RD, 24$^{TH}$ DÁIL (28
FEBRUARY 1973-16 FEBRUARY 1987). SEANAD: 12 AUGUST 1969 -
1973. DID NOT SEEK RE-ELECTION TO THE 25TH DAIL.
EUROPEAN PARLIAMENT: 1979-1981(RESIGNATION)
AGE AT ENTRY TO DÁIL: 32
FAMILY: WIDOW OF DAN DESMOND (TD FOR CORK SOUTH, 1948-61, MID-CORK 1961-4). TWO DAUGHTERS.
MOTHER OF CLLR. PAULA DESMOND, MAYOR OF CORK COUNTY COUNCIL, 2003.
EDUCATION: CONVENT OF MERCY, KINSALE; ST. VINCENT'S SCHOOL, CORK
OCCUPATION: CIVIL SERVANT, DEPARTMENT OF POSTS & TELEGRAPHS, DUBLIN
ADDRESS: MAIN STREET, CARRIGALINE, COUNTY CORK (ADDRESS WHILE IN DÁIL)
PUBLICATIONS: SEE CALLAN, C. AND BARRY DESMOND. IRISH LABOUR LIVES: A BIOGRAPHICAL DICTIONARY OF IRISH LABOUR
PARTY DEPUTIES, SENATORS, MPS AND MEPS. DUBLIN, WATCHWORD, 2010.
DATE OF DEATH: 6 JANUARY 2005. BURIED IN CROSSHAVEN, CO. CORK.

## Career:

Minister for Health and Minister for Social Welfare, June 1981-March 1982.
Member (alternate), New Ireland Forum. Labour Party opposition front-bench
spokesperson on Education 1965-9. Chairperson, Women's Representative
Committee, 1975. Member, Committee on Procedure and Privileges 1965-9;
Dáil and Seanad Standing Joint Committee on Consolidation Bills, 1973.
Member, Joint Committee on Marriage Breakdown, 1983; Member, Joint
Committee on Women's Rights, 1983; Dáil and Seanad Joint Library Committee
1973; Member, European Parliament, 1979-81, elected in the first direct
elections for Munster constituency. Member, Cork County Council, 1965; Cork
County Vocational Education Committee, 1965; Cork Health Authority, 1965-
71.

**Eileen Desmond** was elected to the Dáil in 1965 at a by-election in Mid-Cork caused by the death of her husband whilst both were recuperating from tuberculosis. Her victory in that by-election was a factor in the dissolution of the 17th Dáil. She did not have the opportunity to take her seat, because the Dáil was dissolved by Taoiseach Lemass, of Fianna Fáil, who had declared during the campaign that if Fianna Fáil did not win the seat, he would call a general election. In the ensuing general election she topped the poll in Mid-Cork and was elected. She was defeated in the 1969 general election and in a by-election in 1972. She was again elected in Mid-Cork in the general election of 1973.

As a Deputy, a case she fought on behalf of a woman constituent ended in a major court decision that was instrumental in the establishment of the Family Courts Service. She supported the unsuccessful Contraceptives Bill in 1974.

An influential figure in the Labour Party from the time of her first election, Desmond could have contested the Labour party leadership after the 1981 election. Instead she supported Michael O'Leary, having opposed him in the 1977 leadership election against Frank Cluskey.

As Minister for Health and Social Welfare, Desmond was the first woman to have held a senior cabinet portfolio since the foundation of the State. She was the only woman in that short-lived (eight months) 1981-82 coalition Cabinet. Her Ministerial career was hampered by poor health. Once she was brought on a stretcher from Cork to a Dáil division. Nevertheless, she created the National Combat Poverty Agency, which addressed inequality. She achieved a 25% increase in social welfare allowance, "a level never achieved before or since" (Callan, C. and Barry Desmond. Op.cit. 2010).

She was not appointed to Cabinet in late 1982 as her health was not robust.

In 1983, despite enormous pressure exerted on her to do otherwise, she was the only woman Dáil deputy to vote against the Bill to hold a referendum to insert an anti-abortion clause into the Constitution.

[This amendment inserted in the constitution in 1983 would be the subject of further controversies, court judgments and further referenda and was repealed by a referendum in 2018.]

She was an alternate member of the Labour Party delegation to the New Ireland Forum in 1983–84 at which political parties discussed potential developments that might alleviate the Troubles in Northern Ireland.

> *"She was a woman of enormous personal and political courage. At all times she fearlessly followed her conscience and her political instincts. For her the determining factor was whether a position was right or wrong, not how popular it might prove with the public."*

(Labour Party leader Pat Rabbitte, Irish Times, 7 January, 2005)

# Gemma Hussey, née Moran

DATE/PLACE of BIRTH: NOVEMBER 1938/BRAY, COUNTY WICKLOW
PARTY: FINE GAEL
Constituency: Wicklow. Seanad: National University of Ireland
Dáil/Seanad: 23RD-25TH Dáil (18 February 1982-14 June 1989). Seanad (17
AUGUST 1977-20 APRIL 1982)
AGE AT ENTRY TO SEANAD: 38
AGE AT ENTRY to DÁIL: 42
FAMILY: MARRIED TO DERMOT R. HUSSEY; TWO DAUGHTERS, ONE SON
EDUCATION: ST BRIDGET'S SCHOOL, BRAY; LORETO CONVENT, BRAY; CONVENT OF THE SACRED HEART, MOUNT ANVILLE,
DUBLIN; UNIVERSITY COLLEGE DUBLIN (BA ECONOMICS & POLITICS)
OCCUPATION: FOUNDER DIRECTOR, ENGLISH LANGUAGE INSTITUTE, DUBLIN
Address: Temple Road, Dublin 6

## Career:

Minister for Social Welfare, February 1986-March 1987. Minister for Labour, January-March 1987. Minister for Education, December 1982-February 1986. Fine Gael spokesperson on Education, 1987; Fine Gael spokesperson on Women's Affairs, November 1980-June 1981; Fine Gael spokesperson on Arts, Culture and Broadcasting, 1982. Government Leader of the Senate 1981-82. Member, Joint Oireachtas Committee on the Secondary Legislation of the European Communities, 1977-80 and 1987; Chairperson, 1987. Member, Seanad Committee of Procedure and Privileges 1977-81. Member, Joint Committee on Building Land, 1982. Vice-chairperson, Irish-Arab Parliamentary Association, 1978-82. Committee member, British-Irish Parliamentary Association, 1978-82. Member, Commission of Enquiry into the Penal System, 1979-80. Chairperson, Women's Political Association, 1973-5 (Vice-chairperson, 1975-7), Council for the Status of Women 1973-1975. Founder member. National Women's Talent Bank. Director Abbey Theatre 1974-8. Founder director, TEAM (Children's Educational Theatre). Member, AIM Group; Bray Chamber of Commerce; Dalkey and Bray School Projects; Council for Civil Liberties; Irish Council of European Movement; Mental Health Association of Ireland; Irish Women's Aid; Association for Welfare of Children in Hospital; An Taisce; Children First. Founder Director, European Women's Foundation.

PUBLICATIONS: Hussey, Gemma. At the Cutting Edge: Cabinet Diaries, 1982-1987, Dublin: Gill and Macmillan, 1990; Ireland Today: Anatomy of a Changing State, Viking Penguin/Town House, 1993.

**Gemma Hussey** entered the Senate in 1977 as an Independent with a background in the women's movement. She had been Chair of the Women's Political Association from 1973 to 1975, and a member of the Council for the Status of Women, which published the influential report *Ireland: Status of Women (1977)* outlining the subordinate legal and economic status of women. Though she had joined Fine Gael in 1972, she did not accept the party whip in the Seanad until November 1980.

As a Senator Hussey attempted to have legislation on rape introduced, by sponsoring the *Sexual Offences Bill, 1980,* which lapsed at First Stage. She authored the *Women in Broadcasting in RTÉ* report (1981).

She contested the Wicklow constituency during the 1981 general election, at which time she was the Fine Gael spokesperson on Women's Affairs. In this role she took a cautious approach to divorce and expressed her opposition to abortion. She accompanied party leader Garret FitzGerald to the meeting with a delegation from the Pro-Life Amendment Campaign in which he committed Fine Gael to holding a referendum on the addition of an anti-abortion amendment to the Constitution. In 1983 she campaigned against the addition of this amendment to the Constitution, taking the position that, as a matter of constitutional law, a woman's human rights should not be diminished upon pregnancy.

Hussey took the initiative in opposing the government's decision to close Ardmore Studios in Bray. She suggested that in order to save costs ministerial Mercedes cars be replaced by more modest cars.

She was appointed Minister for Education within a year of her entry into the Dáil. She declined the services of the Department's Press Officer, Frank Dunlop (whose activities as an agent for property developers would later be investigated by the Flood and Mahon tribunals). She began modernising the education system and increasing the importance of the Department of Education. Among the policy discussion papers published under her aegis were *The Ages of Learning*, a discussion paper issued in June 1984, and *Partners in Education* (1985).

The precarious state of public finances meant that much of her time had to be devoted to finding ways of reducing the Education budget. Within weeks of taking office, she introduced charges for the school transport system. Because these affected every townland in the country, this decision was regarded as akin to political suicide, and she was attacked from all sides. She persevered with the measure, although the government decided to exclude from the new charges the children of social welfare recipients.

Between 1980 and 1986, third-level enrolments were increasing rapidly and Hussey secured increased government provision for higher education. At a time of severe spending cutbacks, she justified this on grounds of expanding student numbers. In 1984, as a result of her negotiation of the allocation from the European Social Fund, annual grants of £300 were provided for about a third of school-leavers who undertook employment-preparation courses.

In 1985, Hussey was engaged in a dispute with teachers' unions, whose demands for a pay increase had been rejected by the government. She questioned the morality of so substantial a pay claim at a time of national stringency.

Another controversy arose in 1986. Because primary-school pupil numbers were set to decline, the government decided to close Carysfort Teacher Training College. This information was leaked before the relevant authorities had been informed, and many accusations were made against the Minister for Education. The teachers' dispute was still in progress. Because Hussey occupied a marginal seat, Taoiseach FitzGerald decided to move her in his cabinet reshuffle of early 1986. She had been the most reforming Minister for Education since Donogh O'Malley, having opened up the Department to new ideas and given education a higher profile.

The Taoiseach's plan was to create a new Department of European Affairs for Hussey — a prospect which appealed to her. However, he was informed by the Secretary to the Government that his proposal would entail dividing the Department of Foreign Affairs in two and creating a separate secretariat for the new European Affairs department. A new Department was not created and Hussey was appointed Minister for Social Welfare.

Among the policy discussion papers published under her remit was *Social Welfare - 4 Years of Progress,* 1987.

Late in 1986, she was active in the unsuccessful campaign to secure a Yes vote in the divorce referendum. (In the subsequent referendum in 1995 the electorate voted Yes to divorce). From 1987 to 1989 she was Fine Gael front-bench spokesperson on Education.

Her *Cabinet Diaries,* published in 1990, give a unique and valuable insight into the process of decision-making. A Supreme Court judgment in 1992 placed an absolute obligation on government members to adhere to cabinet confidentiality. Hussey's *Cabinet Diaries* thus attained a special value as any such publications would henceforth be prohibited.

Gemma Hussey did not contest the 1989 general election and retired undefeated from parliament. She continued to be influential in public life into the 21st century through media contributions, in some of which she described how the decisions taken by her government stabilised the public finances and laid the foundation for the recovery known as the 'Celtic Tiger'.

She was shortlisted for European of the Year, 2003 and received the Women Who Make a Difference Award from the International Women's Forum, 2003.

# Mary O'Rourke, née Lenihan

Date/Place of Birth: May 1937/ATHLONE
Party: Fianna Fáil.
Constituency: Dáil – Longford-Westmeath (1982-92; 2007-11); Westmeath (1992-2002). Seanad - Industrial & Commercial Panel, 1981-2. Cultural & Educational Panel, April-November 1982
Dáil: 24th, 25th, 26th, 27th, 28th Dáil (24 November 1982-2002). 30$^{th}$ (2007-2011)
Seanad: 15$^{th}$, 16$^{th}$ (12 August 1981-23 November 1982. 21$^{st}$, 22$^{nd}$ (2002-2007).
Age at Entry to Seanad: 44
Age at Entry to Dáil: 45
Family: Married Enda O'Rourke, two sons. Daughter of P.J. Lenihan, (TD, Longford-Westmeath 1965-70), sister of Brian Lenihan (TD, Roscommon-Leitrim, Dublin West. Tanaiste and Minister in many departments, in office 1957-97), aunt of Brian Lenihan (TD, Dublin West, 1996-2011, Minister) and of Conor Lenihan (TD, Dublin South-West, 1997-2011). Mother of Cllr. Aengus O'Rourke.
Education: St Peter's, Athlone; Loreto Convent, Bray, County Wicklow; University College,Dublin; Maynooth College (BA,H.Dip.Ed.)
Occupation: Secondary teacher.
Address: Arcadia, Athlone, County Westmeath.
Publications: O'Rourke, Mary. Just Mary: a memoir. Dublin, Gill and Macmillan, 2012. O'Rourke, Mary. Letters of my life. Dublin, Gill, 2016. Gunning, Ellen. Capital women of influence. Dublin, Liffey, 2009.

## Career:

Minister for Public Enterprise, 26 June 1997-2002. Minister for Education, 1987-91. Minister for Health, 14 November 1991 - February 1992. Minister of State at the Department of Enterprise and Employment, with special responsibilities for Labour Affairs, 1993-4. Minister of State at the Department of Industry & Commerce (Trade & Marketing), February 1992-January 1993. Leader of the Seanad 2002-2007. Chairperson, Joint Committee on the Constitutional Amendment on Children 2007-2011, Joint Committee on European Affairs, 2007-February 2011; its Sub-Committee on Review of the Role of the Oireachtas in European Affairs, 2010. Member, Joint committee on the Constitution, 2007-2011. Member, Joint Committee on Foreign Affairs, 2002-, its Sub-Committee on Human Rights, 2002-. Member, Joint Committee on House Services, 2002-. Member, Joint Committee on Standing Orders, 2002-

Committee of Selection of Seanad Éireann 2002 – 2007; Seanad Éireann Committee on Procedure and Privileges 2002-. Member, Committee on Members' Interests of Seanad Éireann, 2002-. Member, British-Irish Inter-Parliamentary Body.

Front-bench spokesperson on Enterprise and Employment, 1995-7. Deputy Leader, Fianna Fáil, 1994. Member, Joint Committee on Women's Rights, 1983; on Small Business and Services, 1995. Member, Forum for Peace and Reconciliation, 1997. Member, Westmeath County Council, 1987-. Member, Athlone Urban District Council, 1974-87 (chairperson 1980-81, 1984-5 and 1986-7).

**Mary O'Rourke** was first elected to the Dáil in November 1982 for Longford-Westmeath, which she represented until boundary revisions in 1992, and for Westmeath thereafter. She and her brother, Brian Lenihan, became the first sister and brother to serve in the same Cabinet, the twenty-first Government, appointed on 12 July 1989. They served together until 31 October 1990.

O'Rourke recalled childhood political influences:

> *One particular occasion stands out in my mind — I think it must have been the general election of 1948 — when Eamon de Valera came to Athlone to address a huge rally…. I was eleven years of age, and was allowed with my three siblings to go to hear de Valera. He came to visit our house afterwards and Brian, Paddy and Ann were allowed to join with all the Party faithful in animated discussion and chat in the 'big room'…. I was packed off to bed amid howls of anger and no cajolery would pacify me….*
>
> *Up the corridor I could hear the loud talk, the laughter, the argument growing more tense as time went on. Nothing would do me but to be part of it. I got myself a cushion and plonked myself outside the door, listening, listening, listening. If I close my eyes now, I can still see myself, the dark corridor, the soft cushion, the closed door, the gaiety, the warmth, the excitement which seemed*

*to be beyond that door and I not part of it. Oh, how I longed to be in the middle of that mysterious grown-up world of politics! Forty-five years on, that memory is still strong and vibrant. For me, it was the start of a long love affair with politics and I'm still enraptured, enthusiastic and enthralled.*

Power. S. (ed.), THOSE WERE THE DAYS, Dublin: Gill and Macmillan, 1995

In 1983 O'Rourke declined an offer of appointment to the shadow cabinet as (junior) minister for Women's Affairs shadowing junior minister Nuala Fennell. She accepted Education instead. She later clarified: "I like Nuala Fennell and thought she was a fine, normal person, particularly for someone in Fine Gael" (*The time of my life*. Irish Times 12 May 2018).

While Minister for Education, she initiated the Applied Leaving Certificate qualification for less academic pupils. She initiated a review of the Leaving Certificate and set up a group to review the primary curriculum. She completed the abolition of the distinction between vocational schools and secondary schools by establishing a single junior-cycle examination, the Junior Certificate, and equalised vocational and secondary schools' pupil-teacher ratios. She abolished the matriculation examination and interviews as means of selecting third-level students.

As the first Minister for Education to challenge the Catholic Church's influence on education, O'Rourke implemented the Stay Safe programme in primary schools. When Stay Safe was opposed by an array of right-wing groups, she enlisted support from parents, teachers and managers. She was regarded by the teaching profession as one of the best Ministers for Education in recent decades. She was embroiled in controversy from 1987 to 1989 over the purchase of Carysfort College lands by the State.

In February 1992, she contested the Fianna Fáil leadership with Albert Reynolds and Michael Woods, and won six votes. Dropped from Cabinet when Reynolds became party leader, she was appointed Minister of

State at the Department of Industry and Commerce (Trade and Marketing) in February 1992. This demotion hit hard:

*I couldn't believe it.... That struck me right in the stomach. I talked, shouted, cried and drank that night. I wept so much, I had the duvet over my head and ranted again all night with Enda.*

*IRELAND ON SUNDAY,* 17 May 1998

She was appointed Deputy Leader of Fianna Fáil in 1994 when Bertie Ahern became its leader.

As Minister for Public Enterprise, her remit covered transport, energy and communications, including telecommunications infrastructure, e-commerce and semi-state agencies. She had responsibility for connecting Ireland to the information superhighway by moving from the old telephone system to a costly high-bandwidth future. Lack of competition was stunting the development of broadband infrastructure and keeping Internet charges too high to allow the growth of e-commerce. In May 1998, she stripped the state telecoms monopoly, Telecom Éireann, of its special EU exemption, which let Ireland avoid a deregulated telecoms market until 2000. Her department published a framework document on encryption.

She was quoted in the *Guardian*:

*There's no point in keeping pace with whatever's happening in other countries. You have to dream, think and articulate what isn't even yet believable in this country* (10 September 1998).

She established an extraordinary Advisory Committee for Telecommunications, which included such experts as Vint Cerf, referred to as the "father of the internet".

O'Rourke managed to have implemented several of the Advisory Committee's recommendations, not least that Ireland should establish a public/private partnership approach to encourage investment and be creative about venture capital. This involved a ground-breaking €15 million public-private investment with telecommunications company Global Crossing, which connected Ireland to internet infrastructure by an undersea fibre-optic cable. The government bought half the cable's capacity and sold it at a steep discount to encourage the growth of e-business.

> *"If that one project had not gone through, we'd be in an utterly different Ireland, with greater economic uncertainty. For years (because of the telecoms crash soon after) we'd have struggled with weak internet connectivity and been of declining interest to international business, especially the tech sector....Thanks to O'Rourke's Global Crossing deal, we have the international connectivity that made Ireland an international business and technology hub."*
>
> (Irish Times, 13 June 2019)

In 2000 O'Rourke re-convened the Advisory Committee, which reported in 2002. Some key elements of this report were achieved, such as increased connectivity for researchers and schools, and backing for regional broadband developments. But other excellent proposals for broadband development were not funded.

> *"Almost all of what we did right—or attempted to do right—was instigated by Mary O'Rourke as minister for public enterprise in the 1990s and early noughties, under the guiding hand of her ingenious department secretary Brendan Tuohy. What they tried to do was nothing short of visionary, and at an international scale.....what they were proposing was seen as a global model."*
>
> (Irish Times, 13 June 2019)

Her department also initiated the Joint Communiqué on Electronic Commerce with the United States, signed by the Taoiseach and President Clinton in September 1998. Full telecommunications liberalisation took place on 1 December 1998. She introduced the Electronic Commerce Bill in April 2000 to give the Republic the strongest legal framework internationally, ahead of the US framework, intending to give the State a competitive advantage. This protected the use of encryption. She deregulated the electricity market with the *Electricity Regulation Act, 1999.*

Despite unprecedented levels of investment in transport infrastructure, problems remained. O'Rourke oversaw a rescue plan for Aer Lingus, addressed long-running industrial action in Iarnróid Éireann, had her plan for state airports company Aer Rianta privatisation blocked by Cabinet, and gave the go-ahead for Dublin's Luas tram system.

In July 1999 she privatised Telecom Éireann to become Eircom in the state's biggest privatisation of a state company. By June 2000, a fall in the Eircom share price meant that 488,000 people who invested in Eircom's flotation had a 27 per cent loss in their investment (*Irish Times*, 23 June 2000). There was speculation that this may have damaged her politically.

In early 2001 she was lampooned in newspaper advertisements by Ryanair CEO Michael O'Leary annoyed at her refusal to break up Aer Rianta and thereby reduce airport charges for his airline. She was vindicated in 2004 when the European Commission ruled that similar financial incentives obtained from the Walloon regional government were in breach of EU common market rules.

There was astonishment when she lost her Dáil seat in the 2002 general election. She had warned the party that their imposition of a vote-splitting strategy would cost her the seat.

> *"I think the world and his mother knows that Bertie [Ahern, Taoiseach] did me, he shafted me....because they laid out what area I could go into and couldn't go into."* (Gunning, Ellen. Capital women of influence. Dublin, Liffey, 2009).

As a "love expert", she became a panellist in 2003 on the TV game show *The House of Love.*

Nominated to the Upper House by the Taoiseach, she became Leader of the Seanad. She insisted on respect for the Seanad by declining to rush legislation without proper debate. She pressed for reforms of the immigration system and campaigned against the deportation of asylum-seekers.

In a speech deploring the fact that the Stay Safe programme introduced while she had been Minister of Education was not available in every school, she recalled resistance to Stay Safe:

> *"I received several letters from bishops and parents saying the programme should be cancelled and that I was on the road to sodomy. I was not on the road to sodomy but others were."*

> (Ferns Report: Statements. Seanad Éireann, Vol.181 No.16, 10 November 2005).

During a debate on the case of an obstetrician who removed women's healthy wombs she expressed empathy by revealing a personal experience:

> *'One man in Athlone who was not particularly nice used to say to me if I happened to meet him: "No child yet. There is a clocking hen in every family". I have never forgotten him. He took delight from the fact that I had not become pregnant [yet]. I can imagine what these women felt....'*

> (Seanad Éireann - Volume 182 - 09 March, 2006. Lourdes Hospital Inquiry: Statements.)

She regained her Dáil seat in the 2007 general election.

> *"I'm so satisfied at having got back my seat....There's nothing to beat democracy."*
>
> (Gunning, Ellen. Capital women of influence. Dublin, Liffey, 2009).

As a member of the Dáil during the financial crisis she supported her nephew Brian Lenihan Jnr., who was Minister for Finance while the government was agreeing to a bailout in 2010 from the troika of the International Monetary Fund, European Central Bank and EU. She described the time:

> *"There was drama, tragedy, pathos, comedy, farce, love and death. It was like a Shakespearean drama."*
>
> (Lee, John and D. McConnell. Hell at the gates. Cork, Mercier, 2016).

O'Rourke was among prominent Fianna Fáil members defeated in the 2011 general election.

She was shortlisted for its accolade of Senator of the Year 2005 by Magill magazine.

# Niamh Bhreathnach

Date/Place of Birth: June 1945/Dublin
Party: Labour
Constituency: Dún Laoghaire
Dáil/ Seanad: 27th Dáil (25 November 1992-5 June 1997); Seanad: 13 June-
5 August 1997 (Taoiseach's nominee, casual vacancy)
Age at Entry to Dáil: 47
Family: Married to Tom Ferris. One daughter, one son
Education: Sion Hill School, Blackrock, County Dublin; Froebel Teacher Training
College, Blackrock
Occupation: Remedial teacher
Address: Blackrock, County Dublin

## Career:

Minister for Education, 12 December 1993-26 June 1997 (resigned on 17 November 1994 on change of government, portfolio reassigned on 18 November 1994). Member, Dublin County Council 1991-January 1993; Dun Laoghaire Borough Council 1991-1 January 1993; Dún Laoghaire-Rathdown County Council, 1999. Vice-chairperson Labour Party, 1989-90. Chairperson Labour Party 1990-January 1993. Chairwoman, Labour Women's National Council. Founder member and Chairperson, Carysfort Area Residents' Association; Blackrock Combined Residents' Association; Booterstown Community Council. Executive member, Dún Laoghaire An Taisce. Member, SIPTU; Maritime Museum Friends; Uniferm (Ireland). Patron, Blackrock Athletic Club. Served two terms on Women's Political Association. Member, Board for the Employment of the Blind.

**Niamh Bhreathnach** was elected on the first occasion on which she contested a Dáil seat. In January 1993 she was appointed Minister for Education, the first woman to be appointed to Cabinet immediately after election to the Dáil (and one of only six people ever appointed thus).

*"The culture in Leinster House was very male. It was lonely being a*

*woman there. In my time I think they introduced scones and tea in the Dáil bar - when you think of it - tea and scones, or a biscuit, in the bar was a bit revolutionary 25 years ago,"* Bhreathnach recalls.

(Irish Independent, 26 November 2017).


As Minister for Education, Bhreathnach published the first White Paper on Education, *Charting our Education Future* (1995), introduced the Leaving Certificate Applied programme, and made Transition Year available to all second-level schools. She also initiated the *Breaking the Cycle* programme, which provided extra teachers and school facilities for rural and urban schools in disadvantaged areas. This was regarded as a significant achievement by the teaching profession. She launched a national initiative to put computers in schools.

She abolished third-level undergraduate tuition fees. This initiated a debate about how higher education should be funded, but was credited by school principals with opening the possibility of university to pupils who would not heretofore have aspired to third level education. She achieved significant increases in education spending. Regional technical colleges became Institutes of Technology during her tenure.

She introduced the *Education Bill, 1997.* This was the first major piece of education legislation since the Stanley Letter of 1831 (which had introduced free primary education). She brought in the *University Act, 1997,* which makes universities accountable for the public money they receive. Trinity College resisted this move and further legislation was required in 2000 to enable Trinity College to comply with it.

> *"I am absolutely confident that history will record Niamh as one of the two or three best Ministers of Education the country has ever seen."*
>
> (Finlay, Fergus. Snakes and ladders. Dublin, New Island Books, 1998)

# Nora Owen, née O'Mahony

Date/Place of Birth: June 1945/Dublin
Party: Fine Gael
Constituency: Dublin North
Dáil/Seanad: 22nd-24th Dail (11 June 1981-16 February 1987), 26th-28th Dáil (15 June 1989-May 2002)
Age at Entry to Dáil: 36
Family: Married to Brian Owen, three sons. Grandniece of General Michael Collins and of Margaret Collins-O'Driscoll TD, Niece of Sean Collins (TD for West Cork 1948-54, 1961-69), Sister of Mary Banotti (MEP for Dublin, 1984 -2004)
Education: Dominican Convent, Wicklow; University College, Dublin (BSc, Diploma in Microbiology)
Occupation: Industrial chemist
Address: Malahide,County Dublin (while in Dáil).

## Career:

Minister for Justice, 1994-1997. Deputy Leader of Fine Gael, March 1993-. Front bench spokesperson on Enterprise, Trade and Employment, 1997; on Foreign Affairs, 1993-4; and European Affairs, 1994; on Health 1992-3; on Foreign Affairs 1989-92; on Overseas Development, 1982. Chairperson, Joint Committee on Co-operation with Developing Countries, October 1982-January 1987. Member, Dáil Committee on Procedure and Privileges, 1981-7, 1989. Member, British Irish Parliamentary Body, 1991-2. Member, Joint Committee on Enterprise and Small Business, 1997. Member, New Ireland Forum , 1983.

Member, Dublin County Council, 1979, and its North County Committee (Chairperson 1980-81). Chairperson, Fingal Committee of Dublin County Council 1992-3. Chair, Justice Group of the Irish Institute of International and European Affairs.

Patron, Collins 22 Society. Member, Executive of Trocaire, 1987-9. Member, Special Olympics Ireland's Council of Patrons and volunteer in the organisation of the Special Olympics World Summer Games held in Dublin, 2003. Chair, Expert Advisory Group on Development Aid reporting to the Minister for Foreign Affairs and Trade. Chair of the Women, Peace and Security Oversight Group. Vice-President, of the Institute of International and European Affairs (IIEA).

Secretary and volunteer, Malahide information Centre, 1976-80. Member, Malahide Community Council; Ard na Mara Residents Association; editorial committee of *Malahide News*. Vice-President, Railway Preservation Society of Ireland, 2012 - .

**Nora Owen** worked as a chemist with Linson Ltd. in Swords from 1965-72. On joining Fine Gael in 1961, she identified with its social democratic wing, and was invited to stand for election to Dublin County Council in 1979 because of her community involvement.

She was an alternate member of the Fine Gael delegation to the New Ireland Forum in 1983–84 at which Irish political parties discussed potential developments that might alleviate the Troubles in Northern Ireland.

Owen volunteered in Rwanda with Concern in 1994. She took part in parliamentary training in Africa, and in Latvia, Romania, Cambodia, Philippines and Afghanistan. She has a strong record in the struggle against global poverty, and the promotion of human rights, justice and equality.

Her term as Minister for Justice coincided with major problems—an increase in serious crime, a divided police force, overcrowded prisons and an overburdened courts system. She undertook a significant programme of criminal law reform.

Among the major changes she implemented was the referendum on bail on 28 November 1996, leading to the *Bail Act, 1997,* which allows a court to refuse bail to those charged with a serious offence where it is considered necessary to prevent those persons committing a serious offence.

A tipping point was the murder of journalist Veronica Guerin in 1996 by criminals involved in the sale of drugs. In its aftermath Owen introduced the *Criminal Assets Bureau Act, 1996* and founded the Criminal Assets Bureau (CAB), which had notable success in cracking down on organised crime. The CAB has been effective against those involved in the importation and distribution of drugs and has also been effective against corrupt officials and terrorists. The *Disclosure of Certain Information for Taxation and Other Purposes Act, 1996* and the *Proceeds of Crime Act, 1996* were designed to ensure that criminals do not benefit from their ill-gotten gains. The CAB model has been copied by other countries.

Other major changes introduced by her were the *Criminal Justice (Drug Trafficking) Act, 1996*, which allows for detention for up to seven days of suspected drug traffickers, and restrictions on the right to silence.

She also introduced the *Children Act, 1997* which protects children against abuse and outlaws child pornography and trafficking in children. The *Sexual Offences (Jurisdiction) Act, 1996,* dealing with child sex tourism, was a Private Member's Bill which was accepted by Owen subject to extensive amendment.

Another anti-crime measure commenced by Owen was an unprecedented prison-building programme, designed to provide 800 prison places.

The effect of these measures was to restore confidence in law and order.

Several controversies marked her time in Justice, including the failure of her Department to inform a judge that he had been delisted by Cabinet as a judge of the Special Criminal Court. A number of republican prisoners had to be released on Minister Owen's instruction, but were subsequently re-arrested.

As a grandniece of Michael Collins, a signatory of the 1921 Anglo-Irish Treaty, Owen is patron of the Collins 22 Society, founded in 2002 to perpetuate the name and work of Michael Collins.

> *As Minister for Justice (1994–1997), I was part of the team that participated in Anglo-Irish meetings with politicians in the North and the UK. In 1996, as I was being driven into Downing Street to a meeting with Prime Minister John Major, I was daunted and*

*excited by the realisation that I was only the second member, on official business, of the Collins clan to be literally following in the footsteps of Michael Collins 75 years later.*

(National Archives. Treaty Reflection. N.d.)


After losing her Dáil seat in the Fine Gael general electoral débacle in 2002, Owen hosted current affairs programmes on TV, including *Midweek* on TV3.

Of her time in politics Owen said:

> *"It's seductive, I loved it. If I had my time over, I'd do it all again but find the time to stop and smell the roses."*

(Magill, 12 January 2010)

# Mary Harney

DATE/PLACE OF BIRTH: 11 MARCH 1953/ BALLINASLOE, COUNTY GALWAY
PARTIES: FIANNA FÁIL, PROGRESSIVE DEMOCRATS
CONSTITUENCY: DUBLIN SOUTH WEST (JULY 1981-MAY 2002) / DUBLIN MID-WEST (MAY 2002-FEBRUARY 2011)
DÁIL/SEANAD: 22ND-28TH DÁIL (11 JUNE 1981 TO FEBRUARY 2011); TAOISEACH'S NOMINEE TO THE SEANAD (25 AUGUST 1977 – 10 JUNE 1981)
AGE AT ENTRY TO SEANAD: 24
AGE AT ENTRY TO DÁIL: 28
FAMILY: MARRIED BRIAN GEOGHEGAN, 2001.
Education: Mercy Convent, Goldenbridge, Inchicore, Dublin; Coláiste Bhríde, Clondalkin, County Dublin; Trinity College, Dublin BA(Mod))
Occupation: Researcher, Financial institution
ADDRESS: BALLSBRIDGE, DUBLIN 4

## Career:

Tánaiste and Minister for Enterprise, Employment and Trade, June 1997 - 2004. First woman Tánaiste (1997-2006). Minister for Health and Children, 2004-2011. Leader, Progressive Democrats party, October 1993-2006, again from 2007-2008, first woman leader of a national party. Minister for State at the Department of the Environment, with special responsibility for Environmental Protection, 1989-92. Member, Joint Committee on the Secondary Legislation of the European Communities, 1977. Member, Public Accounts Committee, 1982, May 1988. Member, Joint Committee on Marriage Breakdown. Member, Committee on Selection, 1987. Member, Special Committee on the *Judicial Separation and Family Law Reform Bill, 1987,* March 1988. Member, Select Committee for Legislation and Security, 1993-7. Member, Forum for Peace and Reconciliation, 1997. Progressive Democrat spokesperson on Justice and Social Policy, Health and Social Welfare, and party chief whip. Member, Dublin County Council 1979-91, Vice-chairperson, County Dublin Vocational Education Committee 1985.

**Mary Harney** was the first woman auditor of the Historical Society in

Trinity College, where she was active in student politics and joined Fianna Fáil. She thereby came to the attention of Fianna Fáil leader, Jack Lynch, who secured her a party nomination in the Dublin South East constituency at the 1977 election. She was unsuccessful but was nominated to the Seanad by Taoiseach Lynch on 25 August 1977, becoming the youngest member of that House. She was elected to Dublin County Council in 1979. In June 1981, Harney was elected for Fianna Fáil to the Dáil for Dublin South West.

Harney was among the group who had difficulties with CJ Haughey's leadership of Fianna Fáil. She was an ardent supporter of Desmond O'Malley's leadership challenge in October 1982. This stand almost cost her seat, as she polled barely enough votes for a nomination by the local Fianna Fáil organisation the following month. She opposed Haughey again in the February 1983 leadership crisis but accepted the majority decision. During these challenges attempts were made to intimidate her, including a threat on her life. Having lost the party whip after voting in favour of the Anglo-Irish Agreement of 1985, she quit Fianna Fáil. She was instrumental in establishing the Progressive Democrats (PD) party on 21 December 1985.

On the formation of the Fianna Fáil/Progressive Democrats coalition government in 1989, Harney was appointed Minister of State with responsibility for the Office of the Protection of the Environment. She introduced legislation outlawing the sale and use of bituminous fuel in the Dublin area. The ban ended smog, which reduced greatly the incidence of bronchial illness. This was a significant achievement for a junior minister whose senior minister was not supportive of the measure. She established an independent Environment Protection Agency.

She was appointed Deputy Leader of the Progressive Democrats and Spokesperson on Justice, Equality and Law Reform in February 1993. In October 1993 she became leader of the Progressive Democrats — the first woman to lead a party in Dáil Éireann. The party espoused low taxation, de-regulation and limited government intervention in the economy.

In 1993 Harney was chosen as *Irish Independent* Woman of the Year.


As Minister for Enterprise, Trade and Employment, Harney used her powers to initiate thirteen investigations into companies which tribunals had suggested might have breached company law. The officers appointed by her uncovered 'an enormous amount of apparent wrongdoing'. She appointed three inspectors in 1999 to uncover details of the secret Ansbacher accounts which had been used by wealthy Irish people, including some politicians, to evade tax, and report to the High Court. Her role was delicate as she had also to maintain the Coalition arrangement with Fianna Fáil. Two years earlier, when Fianna Fáil had refused to include the Ansbacher accounts within the terms of reference of the Moriarty Tribunal, many people had thought that the details would never come out. 'But they reckoned without the quiet determination of the Tánaiste' (*The Irish Times,* 29 September 1999).

According to her:

> *Politics is not just about winning a seat, but what you do when you have a seat. I do not want a seat in the Dáil at any cost. Principle must come first....*
>
> EVENING HERALD, 23 May 2000


Harney's approval ratings as party leader in opinion polls were always high, but did not translate into electoral support for the party, which declined. Controversies arose on foot of her 1999 holiday in France at the expense of a businessman lobbying to build a new terminal at Dublin Airport, and, in May 2000, on her approval of the nomination of a Supreme Court judge who had been forced to resign, as Vice-President of the European Investment Bank.

As Minister for Enterprise from 1997 to 2004 Harney embraced free-market economic policies and claimed that these played a key role in the boom known as the Celtic Tiger.

> *"Geographically we are closer to Berlin than Boston. Spiritually we are probably a lot closer to Boston than Berlin........When Americans come here they find a country that believes in the incentive power of low taxation. They find a country that believes in economic liberalisation. They find a country that believes in essential regulation but not over-regulation."*

(Mary Harney speaking to the American Bar Association on 21st July 2000).

She was Minister for Enterprise, Trade and Employment at a time when over half a million jobs were created. Her low-tax strategy, implemented in alliance with FF Finance Minister McCreevy, played a significant role in the creation of those jobs.

Arising from concern at revelations about payments made by businessmen to Taoiseach Haughey and other senior politicians, tribunals were established. These led to the activation of the Companies Acts and of investigations by the Department of Enterprise, Trade and Employment, of which Harney, then Progressive Democrats leader, was Minister. She established the Office of the Director of Corporate Enforcement in 2001 to enforce the provisions of the Companies Acts.

She consolidated her leadership of the Progressive Democrats in the 2002 general election by returning to power with double the seats, from 4 to 8, to take a greater Cabinet role.

The PDs' return to office with Fianna Fáil after the 2002 general election would later come to be viewed as a fateful wrong turn. Fianna Fáil won enough seats to govern with the support of Independents. But the PDs accepted Fianna Fáil's offer to continue in coalition, despite lacking political leverage. However, the PDs maintained their identity and escaped a backlash experienced by Fianna Fáil. (Irish Times, 14 February/ 27 December 2003).

From September 2002 her party opposed the Taoiseach's wish for an 80,000-seat stadium, nicknamed the "Bertie Bowl", on the grounds that the €1 billion cost could not be justified. A scaled down stadium was the outcome in 2004. She inaugurated the Personal Injuries Assessment Board (PIAB) in May 2004, to reduce high litigation costs in personal injuries cases and to compensate claimants quickly and cheaply. This was a major reform of the insurance market long opposed by the legal profession.

> *"I have done it to benefit genuine accident victims and, ultimately, all those who have been paying excessive insurance premiums for far too long. For once, the vested interests have to stand back and let the concerns of the consumer take precedence".* (Business and Finance, 31 May 2004).

The cost of insurance premiums fell as a result, and the PIAB soon reported that it delivered the same level of compensation to claimants three times faster and four times cheaper than if they had gone to court (Business World, 13 September 2005). Her reform of the insurance market entailed tighter road safety laws, including the introduction of penalty points for drivers, reform of court procedures and the introduction of a perjury offence for false or exaggerated claims made in personal injury cases.

The PDs suffered electoral reversals in 2004. They lost local authority seats, won 19 local authority seats out of a targeted 60 and fielded no candidates for election to the European Parliament.

Harney was the only minister in recent memory to request the Health portfolio, a department dubbed 'Angola' (a minefield for political careers) by a predecessor. She brought a drive for change and again challenged vested interests.

She embarked on reform of the health service, aiming to improve the accident and emergency service, reduce waiting lists, re-negotiate the medical consultants' contract, and prioritise cancer services and emergency care.

> *"If Harney can't sort out Health, then nobody can."*
>
> (Sunday Tribune, 3 April 2005).

She immediately secured an extra €1 billion for the sector. She defused her first controversy, extralegal nursing home charges, an issue neglected since 1976 by 16 previous administrations. In an attempt to limit the cost to taxpayers, she introduced a bill in December 2004 to legitimise the charges. The retrospective element was rejected by the Supreme Court and a further Act had to be passed.

In December 2006 she published a plan, Fair Deal, for funding the care of nursing home residents. The objective was to end the inequity of the existing system. The Fair Deal nursing home support scheme was a radical approach to funding the long-term care of the elderly. It contained an option for the state to take a share in the equity of a family home in return for paying indefinitely for long-term care, including a charge "beyond the grave" through a levy equal to 10 or 15% of the sale price of their homes. As the plan was likely to be controversial, its introduction in the run-up to an election was regarded as brave. She was known for putting the national interest ahead of narrow political considerations.

Her Health Bill 2006 provided for the establishment of an independent inspectorate for private and public nursing homes. The creation of this body, as part of the Health Information and Quality Authority, was a significant achievement. It established quality standards for the first time and the necessary enforcement, backed with sanctions. The large investment in community care from 2007 onwards helped many older people to remain in their own homes.

She introduced a €70 million plan to improve emergency services and agreed a €1 billion package to fund initiatives for the elderly, whom she identified as her top priority.

In Cabinet, she was instrumental in planning to take local political influence out of the health services and abolish the Health Boards. She implemented the largest health structural reform, the establishment of the Health Service Executive, in 2005. Accused of rushing the legislation, the government was in 2008 forced to redesign the over-centralised structures, and return to a more regionalised approach. She told the *Irish Independent* that reforming the health system would take at least seven years and she wished for a second term to do it. By the end of 2006 there was a decline in reports of overcrowded A&E departments and patients on trolleys.

She initiated a hospital co-location measure in which public and private patients would be treated in different facilities on the same site. The aim of the initiative was to make available approximately 1,000 additional public acute hospital beds for public patients by transferring private activity, with limited exceptions, from public acute hospitals to co-located private hospitals. No capital outlay was required as the beds in the public hospitals were already in place, funded by the Exchequer. Opponents, including opposition parties, the labour movement and some doctors, criticised this as privatisation based on the US model. They said the measure would result in huge subsidies for developers to build private facilities on public hospital grounds, further embedding health inequality. There was a belief among critics that some changes benefited business interests over the interests of patients.

The plan for co-located hospitals was delayed by legal issues, planning delays and difficulties in securing bank finance, as well as lukewarm Health Service Executive support. Co-location was abandoned by the succeeding government.

In June 2005, she postponed the introduction of risk equalisation (cash transfers from health insurers with low risk profiles to those with high risk profiles), for new entrants to the health insurance market. She cited the damage it would do to competition. However she introduced risk equalisation in December and enacted legislation to put the state-owned Voluntary Health Insurance on a more commercial footing. When health insurer BUPA decided to leave the market in 2006 she was accused of not doing enough to stagger the introduction of risk equalisation.

Harney told the *Irish Times* in 2005 that if agreement on a new medical consultants' contract could not be reached by Easter 2006 she would push it through anyway. This did not then happen. She was criticised because of protracted negotiations of a new consultants' contract, the slow rate of improvement in functioning of the Health Service Executive and cancer misdiagnoses. She was described by observers of Health as its "mudguard', deflecting controversy from governing partners Fianna Fáil for difficult political decisions.

Her success in reforming the health service was evident most notably in the new cancer control programme, improved A&E services, a radically new consultants' contract introduced in 2008, and easier means tests for medical cards. Nurse-prescribing was introduced. Regulation of the medical profession was modernised by the *Medical Practitioners Act 2007*, which introduced the new non-medical member majority on the Medical Council. The PD-led National Treatment Purchase Fund was a successful, if expensive, initiative in ending waiting lists for standard surgical procedures for public patients, to the benefit of the private hospital sector. A report by the National Treatment Purchase Fund in April 2010, showed that the average waiting time for public patients for surgical and medical procedures was 2.5 months, the lowest it had ever been.

By 2006 Harney was the longest serving party leader in the Republic, having served for 13 years. When challenged for the leadership in June 2006, she had the unanimous support of the parliamentary party. She resigned as party leader on 7 September 2006.

*"She achieved many firsts for a woman, but it was her courage and conviction which set her apart.* (Irish Times, 8 September 2006).

*"Her 13 years leaves Mary Harney as one of the most successful politicians of her generation. And she will be a hard act to follow."* (Irish Independent, 8 September 2006).

However, her party was decimated in the 2007 election. As one of just two PD TDs returned in 2007, she resumed leadership in the interim until a new leader took office in April 2008. But the party was in terminal decline and was wound up in November-December 2008.

As an Independent, she retained her Health ministerial portfolio, with the confidence of the government.

In the 2009 Great Recession her attempt to introduce a reduction in dispensing fees aimed at reducing public spending was resisted by the Irish Pharmacy Union (IPU). Two years earlier, by court action, the IPU had prevented the Minister for Health from cutting dispensing fees. When new legislation was passed in 2009 the IPU entered a dispute which closed many pharmacies. But it capitulated a fortnight later. A powerful vested interest group had fragmented in the face of government determination to curtail its costs and their profit margin.

*"This time, the groundwork was properly laid and Ms. Harney made no mistakes. Divisions between pharmacists were exploited; the Health Service Executive put special dispensing arrangements in place and fewer than half of all chemists joined in the dispute. The Minister for Health has done well to hold her nerve and to protect the public interest. While she and her department can be blamed for allowing costs to run out of control in the first place, the example set in this confrontation should encourage her Cabinet colleagues to push ahead with other necessary reforms."* (The Irish Times, August 13, 2009).

On 19 January 2011 she announced her intention to stand down at the next election, and also resigned from her ministerial post. By then, in the wake of the financial crash, it had become apparent that neo-liberal economic policies had not served the country as well as had been thought during the boom years, and that 'light-touch' regulation of financial institutions had been a factor in the banking collapse of 2008.

> *"Under her watch it was decided to stop investing in more acute hospital beds in order to tackle access delays, and instead to increase hospital efficiency by providing day-care and community based primary care centres.*
>
> *During her tenure, hospitals across the country were modernised to make all services including cancer services safer, and the newly negotiated consultant contract would in future mean that new consultants would work only in public hospitals. The high cost of drugs in Ireland was also reduced.*
>
> *Some will point out the unacceptably long waits in some emergency departments. While there will always be spikes, because this is the nature of an on-demand service, it must be noted that the majority of hospitals have resolved this issue over the past five years."*
>
> (Brendan Drumm, first CEO of the HSE, Irish Times, 25 January 2011).

> *"Mary Harney centralised cancer services so that they worked and thus improved the health of the nation".*
>
> (John FitzGerald, economist, RTÉ 1 radio, 6 January 2019).

Harney was a senior minister for 14 years, becoming the longest-serving woman minister in the history of the State. She served seven years each as Minister for Enterprise, Trade and Employment and as Minister for Health and Children.

She was shortlisted for Overall Politician of the Year Award 2005 by Magill magazine and for Minister of the Year 2007.

# Síle De Valera

DATE/PLACE of Birth: DECEMBER 1954/DUBLIN
PARTY: FIANNA FÁIL
CONSTITUENCY: Dublin Mid-County (1977-81), CLARE (1987-2007)
DÁIL/SEANAD: 21ST DÁIL (16 June 1977-11 June 1981), 25TH-29TH DÁIL
(17 FEBRUARY 1987-2007)
AGE AT ENTRY to DÁIL: 22
FAMILY: GRANDDAUGHTER of EAMON DE VALERA (PRESIDENT of IRELAND, 1959-73; TAOISEACH,
1937-48, 1951-4, 1957-9; PRESIDENT of THE EXECUTIVE of THE IRISH FREE STATE 1932-7;
PRESIDENT, 1ST DÁIL, 1919-21. TD for CLARE, 1918-61. PRESIDENT, 2ND DÁIL, 21 JANUARY 1922).
COUSIN of EAMON Ó CUIV (TD, GALWAY WEST, 1992-, MINISTER of STATE for GAELTACHT AND THE ISLANDS,
July 1997-2002)
EDUCATION: LORETO CONVENT, FOXROCK, COUNTY DUBLIN, UNIVERSITY COLLEGE DUBLIN (BA, H.DIP .ED.,
DIP. IN CAREER GUIDANCE, D PSYCH.SCI.)
OCCUPATION: CAREER GUIDANCE TEACHER
ADDRESS (WHILE IN OFFICE): TULLA ROAD, ENNIS, CO. CLARE

## Career:

Minister for Arts, Heritage, Gaeltacht and the Islands, June 1997-2002. Minister of State at Department of Education and Science, responsible for adult education, youth affairs and educational disadvantage, 2002-December 2006. Fellow, Harvard University Institute of Politics and Kennedy School of Government, Spring 2008 (lecturer on European integration and EU-US relations). Fianna Fáil front-bench spokesperson on Arts, Culture & Heritage, 1995-7. Member, Committee on Procedure and Privileges, 1977; Joint Committee on the Secondary Legislation of the European Communities, 1977; Joint Committee on Women's Rights, 1987-9, 1989-92; Joint Committee on Employment, 1992; Select Committee on Social Affairs, April 1993; Select Committee on Legislation and Security, 1993-7. Member of European Parliament, 1979-84, and of its Committees for Social Affairs and Employment, Youth, Education and Sport and the Ad Hoc Women's Committees.

**Síle De Valera** was the youngest member of the Dáil at her election in 1977. She contested Dublin South in 1981 and February 1982, and the constituency of Clare in November 1982. In her early career she called for a British withdrawal from Northern Ireland and a government demonstration of republicanism. She visited Bobby Sands in prison and criticised Margaret Thatcher's handling of the H-Block hunger strikes.

*If our political leaders are not seen to be furthering our republican aspirations through constitutional means, the idealistic young members of our community will become disillusioned... and turn to violence to achieve their aims.*

SPEECH AT Liam Lynch commemoration at Fermoy, County Cork, seen as challenge to leadership of Jack Lynch.

*THE IRISH TIMES,* 10 September 1979

De Valera resigned the Fianna Fáil whip in July 1993 in protest against the government's removal of the obligatory stopover for transatlantic flights at Shannon Airport, County Clare. She rejoined the party in 1994. In December 1994, Taoiseach Ahern appointed her front bench spokesperson on Arts and Culture.

Her remit as Minister for Arts and Heritage included Ireland's régime for writers and composers, a growing film industry, and the music industry. She introduced the *Broadcasting Act, 2001* — the first major piece of legislation in the area for more than a decade — to introduce digital television, provide for thirty-five channels, define public service broadcasting and aid the Irish film industry.

The Minister sought to address issues raised by the market, by social and cultural demands, and by viewers.

*Other countries in Europe are standing back and saying 'Let's see how it develops.' I don't think we have the luxury of that... Obviously digitalisation brings a completely new era of technology*

*— it is a very exciting one and it means great change and great choice. But we have to ensure that our own cultural identity isn't lost in this morass.*

THE IRISH TIMES, 11 June 1999


De Valera introduced the *Broadcasting (Major Events Television Coverage) Act, 1991,* to ensure that the public could continue to watch the most important sporting contests on ordinary television. The GAA expressed concern that the proposed law could deny it the right to get the best price for the television rights to its games, but she believed that the citizens' rights must be safeguarded.

She extended the Section 35 tax break for the film industry from 1999 to 2000, and set up the Film Industry Strategic Review Group which reported in 1999.

A speech given by De Valera in 2000 in Boston about her fear of closer EU integration occasioned surprise. Expressing the hope that Ireland would "exercise a more vigilant, a more questioning attitude to the European Union", she asserted that "directives and regulations agreed in Brussels can often seriously impinge on our identity, culture and traditions." Also she said that the bureaucracy in Brussels didn't always "respect the complexities and sensitivities of member-states." Hitherto, Ireland, as a beneficiary of EU transfers, was regarded as supportive of the European Union. Here was a first suggestion that elements of the electorate might chafe under the conditions to be met. This factor would become salient in the rejections of the Nice I Treaty (2001) and Lisbon I Treaty (2008) which extended the powers of the EU. Her speech stimulated a debate on whether Ireland's economic and social values were closer to those of the US or the EU, "Boston or Berlin". This theme was taken up by another minister, Mary Harney (qv). (The Nice and Lisbon Treaties were later passed by the Irish electorate).

In cabinet, De Valera provided a legislative framework for the Arts and also the Heritage Fund, ensuring that important historic documents stayed in the country. Her strong support enabled the acquisition and display of the Eileen Gray collection at the National Museum and archive.

There was opposition in some quarters to her handling of the Arts and tension between her and the board of the Abbey Theatre over its future location.

*"She has engaged in some public slagging of the Irish Times following criticism in the paper of her handling of the arts, which has done her no harm at all with the party faithful."*

(Sunday Tribune, April 21, 2002).

Broadcasting policy was controversial during her tenure. In 2001 she granted RTÉ an increase in the licence fee of less than half what it had sought.

*"Had it not been for the determination of Síle de Valera, [RTÉ] would be on the verge of collapse. Her refusal to hand over a large licence fee increase without substantive financial reform has at least forced some degree of accountability and openness on a broadcaster that revelled in secrecy".*

(Sunday Independent, 13 July 2003).

*"Senior executives may reflect that the delay in granting an increase may have saved them from themselves. For example, plans to embark on a potentially disastrous expansion into new digital channels were shelved due to lack of finances".*

(Irish Times, 14 December 2002).

While Minister of State at Education, she made adult education her priority. She set up the Council for Further Education and the Educational Disadvantage Committee in 2004. Investment in adult literacy reached its highest level; more than 31,000 adults received tuition.

She announced in 2005 that she would retire at the 2007 election. She stepped down from her ministerial post on 8 December 2006, thereby ending the De Valera name in the Dáil (though not the dynasty). She said she had kept notes and intended to write memoirs.

After her retirement from parliament she lectured on European integration and EU-US relations while a Fellow of Harvard University Institute of Politics and Kennedy School of Government, Spring 2008.

# Mary Coughlan

DATE/PLACE OF BIRTH: MAY 1965/CRANNY, INVER, COUNTY DONEGAL
PARTY: FIANNA FÁIL
CONSTITUENCY: DONEGAL SOUTH WEST
DÁIL/SEANAD: 25TH, 26TH, 27TH, 28TH, 29TH, 30TH DÁIL (17 FEBRUARY 1987-FEBRUARY 2011)
AGE AT ENTRY TO DÁIL: 21
FAMILY: DAUGHTER OF CATHAL COUGHLAN (TD, DONEGAL SOUTH WEST, 1983-6); NIECE OF CLEMENT COUGHLAN (TD, DONEGAL SOUTH WEST, 1980-83). Married to David Charlton; one daughter, one son. Education: Ursuline Convent, Sligo; University College Dublin, (BSoc Sci.)
OCCUPATION: SOCIAL WORKER

## Career:

Tánaiste and Minister for Education and Skills, 23 March 2010-March 2011. Tánaiste and Minister for Health, 20 January 2011-March 2011. Tánaiste and Minister for Enterprise, Trade and Employment, May 2008 - 22 March 2010. Appointed (first woman) Minister for Agriculture and Food in the reshuffle of 29 September 2004 - 7 May 2008. Minister for Social and Family Affairs, June 2002-September 2004. Minister of State at Department of Arts, Heritage, Gaeltacht and the Islands, February 2001- June 2002.

Spokesperson on Educational Reform 1995-7. Member, Special Committee on the Judicial Separation and Family Law Reform Bill, 1987, 1988. Member, Special Committee on the Recognition of Foreign Adoptions Bill, 1990. Member, Dáil Select Committee on Crime, 1992. Chairperson, Joint Committee on the Irish Language, 1993-5. Vice-Chairperson, Joint Committee on Tourism, Sport and Recreation, 1997. Member, Joint Committee on Employment, 1992; on Women's Rights, 1992; on the Irish Language, 1987. Member, Donegal County Council, 1986; Donegal County Vocational Education Committee, 1986 (chairperson 1991-2). Chairperson, Board of Management, Abbey Vocational School, Donegal. Member, Board of Management, Killybegs Tourism College. Honorary Secretary, Fianna Fáil party, 1995. Member of British-Irish Parliamentary Body, 1991-2, 1997. President, Killybegs Coast and Cliff Rescue Service.

**Mary Coughlan** was the first woman to represent Donegal in the Dáil.

She told a conference that she had two "election babies" (during election campaigns). (Speech to 'Politics Needs Women' conference, Department of Justice and Equality, 14 December 2018). In 1999 she gave birth to her second child while her husband, a member of the Garda Síochána, recovered from a car crash which resulted in the amputation of his leg. She was still present for most Dáil divisions.

She served as a backbencher for 14 years before her promotion to junior ministerial office in 2001. Coughlan was the junior minister most admired by TDs interviewed for a radio series (Irish Times, 24 April 2002).

Reflecting on her political experiences, she said

> ".....Politics is a very difficult job..... It has had a bad reputation, which has been very demoralising for some. But at the same time I love it, there is an adrenalin flow from what you can do.....You have to work very hard in your own constituency. It is very difficult to do if you are very involved in legislation, or at a ministerial level... Clinics, the meetings, being available, attending funerals, attending all the functions, all that is very important. At the same time you have to get a balance, because a lot of people have moved slightly beyond that, and they like their public representative to be articulate, to hear their views expressed during the legislative process, they like them to be involved in the media. Now that does help!"

(Sunday Independent, 10 October, 2004).

While Minister for Social and Family Affairs, she pioneered automatic child benefit for mothers of newborns, established the Family Support

Agency, introduced Personal Retirement Savings Accounts to increase workers' pension cover and oversaw the spending of a record €11.2 billion on social welfare in 2004. Nevertheless, she was unable to defend her department from budget cuts introduced by the Department of Finance in 2003. She was attacked over welfare allowances' cuts, dubbed the "savage 16", especially a reduction in the entitlements of widow/ers. This cut was reversed in 2004.

At Agriculture and Food she committed to safeguarding competition, the live trade and the safest food for consumers (Farmers Journal, 9 October 2004). In an early test, the restructuring of the EU milk quota scheme, she was applauded by farm leaders for reducing the cost of quota (Irish Independent, 4 January 2005). She supported small farmers, despite the Irish Farmers' Association's contention that funding should be directed towards farms best equipped to survive. She appointed Angela Kennedy as Irish Food Board chair, a decision she described as recognition for the role of women and farmers' wives. She introduced the Single Farm Payment, a Common Agricultural Policy reform which Ireland was first to implement. She was unable to prevent an interim agreement, reached at the World Trade Organisation (WTO) trade liberalisation talks, to end farm export subsidies by 2013. The IFA said this would cost up to 50,000 farming jobs, destroy a third of farm output and result in the loss of €1.2 billion to the rural economy. However, exporters said the gains would outweigh the losses long term.

During WTO talks in which Irish agriculture was threatened by attacks on EU farm subsidies and free access to EU markets, she formed an alliance with French ministers to resist the proposals.

The farmers' lobbies praised her for the €8.7bn. she wrested for agriculture from the National Development Plan before the 2007 election, the 60% grants she secured (70% in border counties) under the Farm Waste Management Scheme and the €80-per-cow suckler scheme (Sunday Tribune, 26 October 2008).

Her term as Tánaiste/Minister for Enterprise, Trade and Employment commenced in 2008 during the Lisbon Treaty referendum campaign. Within months the global financial crisis and Great Recession were under way. Arguing in favour of the Lisbon Treaty, she erred in saying that the larger member states still had two Commissioners. The gaffe boosted the No campaign's contention that people should not vote Yes for something they did not understand. She withdrew from the government's doomed Yes campaign. Unemployment rose rapidly. She bore the brunt of anger at 2,100 computer jobs lost at Dell, which was seen as a failure of government policy. In 2009 she was criticised for her handling of revelations of maladministration at the FÁS employment and training agency and the severance package offered to its director general. One of her junior ministers, on demotion to the backbenches, publicly criticised her and government policy.

She acted to close loopholes in company law in order to prevent bank directors from concealing debts owed to the bank. She strengthened the powers of the Director of Corporate Enforcement to enforce more stringent company law provisions.

She received a negative press. Some media claimed she had become the lightning rod for an unpopular government.

> *"Coughlan may not have performed well in the last 12 months, but she's hardly alone. She doesn't deserve to be the sole sacrificial lamb. As the [2009 local and European] election results showed, most voters want the entire cabinet to be axed."*
>
> (Sunday Tribune, June 14, 2009).

By March 2010 opposition women TDs were rallying to her defence. Labour TD, Kathleen Lynch said on radio:

> *"I have to say that I find it personally very difficult to listen to people criticise her in the manner that they do and I think that there just is -- I think there is a little bit of sexism there too. I*

*am not certain that type of criticism would occur if it were a man."*

The *Sunday Tribune* tried to contact the other 32 women TDs and senators (excluding Coughlan and Mary Harney, who was in New Zealand). Of the 29 contacted, 20 (69%), agreed with Lynch, and nine (31%) disagreed. Labour's deputy leader Joan Burton TD (q v) said,

> *"There are lots of male ministers who are not exactly star performers, but they do not generate the same invective that is generated towards her".*

Fine Gael's Senator Fidelma Healy-Eames told the newspaper that it was "regularly said to me in Galway West that a woman does not have to be as good as a man in politics, we have to be twice as good, and I think that is the case for women in politics."

The newspaper maintained:

> *"A fairly common view is that, while she is not the bungler she is being portrayed as in some quarters, her talents and warm, easy manner are much more suited to the Department of Agriculture, where she was very well regarded, than to the more senior Enterprise, Trade and Employment ministry, which requires more subtlety, nous and diplomacy, particularly in dealings overseas."*

> (Sunday Tribune, March 14, 2010).

In December 2010 she announced that she would retire from politics at the next election "for family reasons". She retired undefeated when her service ended after the general election of February 2011.

# Mary Hanafin

DATE/PLACE of Birth: JUNE 1959/THURLES, COUNTY TIPPERARY

PARTY: FIANNA FÁIL

CONSTITUENCY: DUN LAOGHAIRE

DÁIL/SEANAD: 28$^{TH}$, 29$^{TH}$, 30$^{TH}$ DÁIL (6 JUNE 1997 -2011)

AGE AT ENTRY TO DÁIL: 38

FAMILY: MARRIED TO EAMON LEAHY. DAUGHTER OF DES HANAFIN (SENATOR, 1969-93, 1997 -2002);

GRANDDAUGHTER OF CLLR. JOHN HANAFIN (SINN FÉIN, LONGFORD URBAN DISTRICT COUNCIL, TIPPERARY NORTH RIDING COUNCIL; founder member of FIANNA FÁIL). SISTER OF JOHN HANAFIN (SENATOR 2002-11).

EDUCATION: PRESENTATION CONVENT, THURLES; ST PATRICK'S COLLEGE, MAYNOOTH; DUBLIN INSTITUTE OF TECHNOLOGY (BA, H. DIP ED; DIPLOMA in LEGAL STUDIES)

OCCUPATION: SECONDARY SCHOOLTEACHER

ADDRESS: RATHGAR, DUBLIN 6

## Career:
Councillor, Dún Laoghaire-Rathdown, 2014-2019, 2019-. Contested Dún Laoghaire for Fianna Fáil in the 2016 general election. Minister for Tourism, Culture and Sport, 23 March 2010-March 2011. Minister for Enterprise, Trade and Innovation, 20 January 2011-March 2011. Minister for Social and Family Affairs, 7 May 2008-22 March 2010. Minister for Education and Science, 29 September 2004-6 May 2008. Minister of State at the Departments of Health and Children, at Justice, Equality and Law Reform; and at Education and Science, with responsibility for Children, 2000-2002. Minister of State at the Departments of the Taoiseach, with responsibility as (first woman) Government Chief Whip and for Information Technology policy; and Minister of State at the Department of Defence, June 2002-September 2004.

Member, Joint Committee on Broadcasting and Parliamentary Information, 2002-. Member, Joint Committees, Heritage and the Irish language; Justice, Equality and Women's Rights; Education and Science, 1997-. Candidate in the Dublin South East constituency in the 1989 general election.

Member, Dublin City Council, 1985-91; City of Dublin Vocational Education Committee, 1985-91. Member, Senate of the National University of Ireland, 1988. Member, National Executive, Fianna Fail, 1980. Joint Honorary Treasurer of

Fianna Fáil, 1993. Board Member, Dublin Institute of Technology; City of Dublin Youth Services Board. Chairperson, College of Catering. Vice-president CENYC - European Youth Council. Organiser, Co-operation North youth exchanges. Stagiaire scholarship to European Parliament. Robert Schuman silver medal for services towards European unity. Member, Blackrock Historical Society. Secretary, Board of Visitors of the National Museum. Ball de Bhord Gael Linn. Member, Board for the Employment of the Blind. Director, National Building Agency.

**Mary Hanafin**, daughter of a Fianna Fáil senator and granddaughter of a councillor, had a childhood immersed in politics.

*"I used to canvass the nuns in primary school, so I think I was always heading for some sort of political life".*

(Sunday Business Post, 24 April 2005).

While a school pupil she delivered her maiden speech to an audience of university students at the 1975 Fianna Fáil Youth Conference (ibid).

She made her mark as a backbencher by defending tough government decisions, such as the tax individualization introduced in the 2000 Budget. This was unpopular with couples where a spouse was full-time in the home. While first woman Chief Whip, responsible for securing government business, she fielded backbenchers' public complaints about poor party results in the 2004 local and European elections.

Hanafin was appointed Minister of State at the Department of Health and Children in the government reshuffle of 27 January 2000.

As Minister for Children, she initiated the Dáil na nÓg platform, the National Children's Strategy, and the development of playgrounds.

'It wouldn't have done Bertie Ahern any harm at all if he had taken more heed of Mary Hanafin on the contribution of women to public policy *"More women in power would mean more créches, more playgrounds and fewer lap-dancing clubs."'*

(Irish Independent, 20 October 2005).

As Minister for Education she dropped her predecessor's controversial proposals to re-introduce third-level fees. She introduced national testing of primary pupils. In 2005 she announced vastly increased staffing and funding for children with special needs. By 2008 6,000 additional teachers and special needs assistants had been appointed, bringing the special education staff to about 19,000. The National Council for Special Education was established with more than 80 special educational needs organisers. The number of educational psychologists was increased, with the aim of having a service in all schools by 2009/2010. The Irish National Teachers Organisation credited Hanafin with doing more than any of her predecessors on special needs (Irish Times 25 March 2008).

She started the Delivering Equality in Schools (DEIS) school scheme to tackle disadvantage, and provided 300 new posts. This scheme increased the numbers of disadvantaged pupils proceeding to higher education. The number of language support teachers in primary schools increased from fewer than 150 in 2002 to more than 1,500 in 2008.

She supported proposals to reform the Leaving Certificate and introduced curriculum changes in Irish, Maths and Technology.

She initiated the largest investment programme for third level education in the State's history, delivering €1 billion to fund 35 major building projects and a Strategic Innovation Fund. She supported management reforms at third level.

She was credited with lifting teacher morale; publication of school inspection reports; development of a new patronage model for primary schooling; reforms to address school discipline problems, a new emphasis on oral skills in Leaving Certificate Irish, reform of medical education involving new postgraduate courses and expansion of postgraduate education.

But the financial crash of 2007-8 meant that she was unable to deliver commitments on reduction of class sizes and on autism services.

*"She was more knowledgeable and more articulate than most of her predecessors in Education. And her record compares well with the best"* (Irish Times, 13 May 2008).

As Minister for Social and Family Affairs Hanafin implemented cuts, and cracked down on fraud. She abolished an independent agency, Combat Poverty, which had highlighted the depths and effects of poverty, by subsuming it into her Department.

In November 2010 she announced her intention to contend for the leadership of Fianna Fáil once a vacancy arose.

Asked if the old boys' club was ready for a lady leader, Hanafin conceded: *"I'm ready to lead them. The question is whether they're ready for me to lead them.*

(Irish Independent, January 27, 2011).

In the Fianna Fáil leadership contest on 26 January 2011 she came fourth to three male candidates. She was appointed deputy leader of Fianna Fáil on 31 January 2011 and served until March 2011.

She was among prominent Fianna Fáil members who lost their seats in the general election of February 2011.

In 2014 she ruffled party feathers by securing a nomination, against the wishes of the leadership, to run in the 2014 local elections, and was elected. She was again elected in 2019 to Dún Laoghaire-Rathdown Council.

In August 2017 she was appointed to the Forum on Parliamentary Privilege, which examined the balance between freedom of debate for Dáil Members and the rights of individuals. The Forum reported in December 2017.

In the 2016 general election Hanafin contested Dún Laoghaire and was defeated by her former history pupil, Maria Bailey TD (FG), who said

> "She sent me a lovely text afterwards. She said she was very proud of her past pupil doing so well, which wasn't an easy thing to say..." (Irish Independent, 2 March 2016)


Shortlisted as Communicator of the Year in the 2005 Magill Politician of the Year Awards.

Magill Politician of the Year 2005 and 2006.

# Joan Burton

Date/Place of birth: February 1949/South Carlow
Party: Labour
Constituency: Dublin West
Dáil/Seanad: 27th Dáil (25 November 1992-5 June 1997);
29th (2002-7); 30th (2007-11); 31st (2011-2016); 32nd (2016-2020)
Age at entry to Dáil: 43
Family: Married to Cllr.Pat Carroll (Member, DUBLIN County Council);
One daughter.
EDUCATION: SISTERS OF CHARITY, STANHOPE STREET, DUBLIN; UNIVERSITY COLLEGE, DUBLIN (B.COMM, FCA)
OCCUPATION: DUBLIN INSTITUTE OF TECHNOLOGY LECTURER AND CHARTERED ACCOUNTANT
ADDRESS: OLD CABRA ROAD, DUBLIN 7

## Career:
Tánaiste and first woman leader of the Labour Party, 4 July 2014 – 6 May 2016. Minister for Social Protection, 9 March 2011 - 6 May 2016. Minister of State in the Department of Foreign Affairs, 20 December 1994 – 26 June 1997. Member, Joint Committee on Finance and the Public Service, 2007 – 2011. Associate Member, British-Irish Inter-Parliamentary Association. Minister of State at the Department of Social Welfare with special responsibility for poverty, including EU Poverty Plans, and integration of the tax and social welfare codes, 1993-4. Member, Joint Committee on Education and skills 21 July 2016- ; Select Committee on Budgetary Oversight, 21 July 2016- . Select Committee on Arrangements for Budgetary Scrutiny 5 May 2016 -. Member, Dublin County Council, 1991-3. Member, Fingal County Council, 1999-. Delegate, Council for the Status of Women 1988-93. Fellow of the Institute of Chartered Accountants. Member, Teachers' Union of Ireland. Lecturer, University of Dar es Salaam, Tanzania 1983-6, where she worked as part of the Irish Development Co-operation Programme. Deputy leader, Labour Party, 4 October 2007-4 July 2014. Leader, Labour Party, 4 July 2014-20 May 2016. Finance spokeswoman, Labour Party.

**Joan Burton** was first elected to the Dáil in 1992, to represent Dublin West. She had been a candidate in Dublin Central in the 1989 general election.

While a member of Dublin County Council, Burton opposed land re-zonings. In 1993, newspapers quoted her as saying that events in the Dublin County Council chamber provided proof of the need for reform and the disclosure of financial interests by public representatives. In a speech, delivered in County Westmeath, she said:

*"I think the public is entitled to know from each and every councillor what campaign contributions, what hospitality, and what assistance, direct or indirect in recent elections or at any other time they or their parties received from the developers, land owners, associated builders and their agents."*

*IRISH INDEPENDENT,* 22 February 1993

She was accused of libel by forty-two of her former colleagues and threatened with legal action. However, an agent for developers, Frank Dunlop, revealed to the Flood Tribunal on 19 April 2000 that he had made payments to certain members of Dublin County Council. In 2013 the Mahon Tribunal found that several county councillors received corrupt payments from a lobbyist, who set out to bribe them in a bid to rezone land (Irish Independent, 31 July, 2013).

As Minister of State in the Department of Social Welfare from 1993 to 1994, she introduced the back-to-work allowance and other measures to encourage the move from social welfare into employment. As Minister of State in the Department of Foreign Affairs she piloted the *Refugee Act, 1996* through the Dáil.

She lost her Dáil seat in the 1997 election, and was re-elected in 2002.

Burton contested the deputy leadership of the Labour Party in 2002, and in October 2007 was elected deputy leader. She was the first woman Finance spokesperson for a major party in Ireland.

*"Because I have a background as an accountant, I have never been convinced of the value of high marginal rates of tax. I'd prefer to have lower marginal rates but real effective rates which allow people to contribute proportionately with income taxes that are not excessively high".* (Village, June 4th, 2010).

As Opposition Finance spokesperson, she exposed the government's failure to cost the loss to the exchequer of numerous tax reliefs, and consistently highlighted inequalities. Among these were tax shelter schemes used by the wealthy to reduce taxes while modest earners lacked a fair indexation of the income threshold at which they paid higher tax rates. In October 2004 she elicited information that hundreds of the rich, including 11 millionaires, had paid no tax in 2001, by availing of tax shelter schemes (Irish Independent, 1 November 2004). One such scheme, for horse breeding, was found in 2005 to be in breach of EU rules. Her focus on this issue earned her the soubriquet Joan of Arkle from the Irish Independent (4 February 2005). Following her crusade, tax exemptions on stud fees and artists' lucrative works were capped in the Budget of December 2005. The Budget of December 2010 abolished or restricted "many tax reliefs that higher earners use to shelter income unfairly."

She was first to predict that €1bn. in hot money would be raised as part of the Revenue's trawl through Irish residents' foreign bank accounts (Sunday Tribune, 28 March 2004).

In February 2004 she tabled an amendment to the Central Bank and Financial Services Authority Bill 2003 proposing that women and men each comprise at least 40 per cent of the body's board and expert panels. She sponsored the *Ethics in Public Office Bill 2006* to enable the Standards in Public Office Commission to carry out an inquiry on its own initiative without waiting for a complaint.

During the banking crisis of 2008 she was a key influence on the opposition Labour Party policy of nationalising the banks. The

FF/Green/PD government's blanket bank guarantee decision had committed taxpayers to bank rescues costing over €100 billion. As this amounted to three times the national debt before the crisis, that commitment proved controversial. On this decision in September 2008, she commented;

*"I recommended to my colleagues in the Labour Party that if Anglo and Nationwide were the centre of the guarantee, we should not support it. So I recommended very strongly to my colleagues that we shouldn't support the guarantee. I was stunned and we were all stunned to find out in the days following the guarantee that the subordinated debt was included in the guarantee and the bond holders were included in a kind of primary way as well."* (Village, June 4, 2010 ibid.)

Her nationalisation proposal included the intention, once the banks had become solvent, to re-privatise them.

*"The most important thing is that the state sets the terms and conditions under which banks operate."*

She advocated a fund, paid for with a transaction tax on the banks, for any future insolvency problems, to inhibit risky speculation in complex financial instruments such as currency swaps.

*"Down the road the state should seek to recover what taxpayers have put into the banks through a levy,"* she said. *"I'm a strong supporter of a financial transactions tax. The revenue could be used as an insurance or insolvency fund to help pay back some of what the banks have taken."* (Village, June 4, 2010)

Another of her ideas was the extension of the Freedom of Information Act to cover all aspects of the Department of Finance, the Central Bank, Financial Regulator and the National Treasury Management Agency, combined with a "whistleblowers' charter" to protect those who disclose questionable government or private sector practices. (Sunday Tribune, June 20, 2010). In 2014 the *Protected Disclosures Act* was enacted to give protection to all workers who make a protected disclosure.

She condemned the decision of the FF/Green/PD government to apply a lower pay cut to certain senior officials, the result of which, according to Burton, would mean that some of the highest paid public servants' pay would be cut by 3%, while low-paid clerical officers would have their pay cut by 5%.

She noted bias against women deputies by the Ceann Comhairle [Speaker]:

> "There is a problem with how the Ceann Comhairle chairs meetings of the Dáil," she said. "Women really have to be very strong and willing to insist on the right to speak...He is blind to the fact that he calls women very, very late."
>
> (The Herald, 24 May 2010).

Reacting to interruptions during Dáil exchanges, Taoiseach Cowen suggested to Burton's party leader that he "Try and rein her in now and again" (Dáil Éireann Debate, Vol. 722 No. 4.Order of Business 23 November 2010). As Members urged him to apologise, Burton interjected, "The Taoiseach is not going to rein me in....".

After the 2011 general election there was an expectation that Burton would be allocated the Finance portfolio because of her high-profile contributions on finance and the banking crisis. Instead, there was surprise that she received the Social Protection portfolio. At the time, 400,000 people were unemployed. She announced that she would launch an anti-fraud action plan aiming to save the exchequer €625 million in the year ahead. (Sunday Mirror, 25 September 2011).

She acknowledged that she would like to be Taoiseach.

> "I think there's very definitely a role for a woman Taoiseach. I think, for anyone who's asked to be Taoiseach, of course it's the pinnacle of political office and I would certainly like to get

*involved in that job"* (Sunday Mirror, 25 September 2011).


In her first Budget the cuts to Social Welfare were less than anticipated. The cuts of €475 million amounted to some €190 million less than that projected in the previous National Plan. This was seen as a victory for Burton whose department was initially expected to produce cuts of €750 million. (Irish Times, 6 December 2011). She achieved this by the innovation of having employers pay the first four weeks of sick pay and reducing the employers' rebate on redundancy payments from 60% to 30%.

On 28 July 2014 the Economic and Social Research Institute (ESRI) concluded that,

> *"the fiscal policy options chosen by successive governments have contributed to an outcome where inequality in the distribution of income has actually fallen over the last five years. A major factor in ensuring this outcome was the maintenance of the welfare system, broadly unchanged, in the face of the massive increase in numbers depending on it".*

> (ESRI. Research Note on the Distribution of Income and the Public Finances, 2014)


As she distanced herself from the austerity policies of the Government, her personal popularity ratings remained high while the perception of the Government plummeted.

In the wake of disappointing results for Labour in the local and European elections of May 2014, Burton contested the leadership. She was elected leader of the Labour Party on 4 July 2014 by the party membership, the first woman Labour leader in its 102-year history, and was appointed Tánaiste in the Fine Gael/Labour Coalition government.

*"There is a saying in Swahili that women hold up half of the sky."* (Tánaiste Burton Leaders' Questions, Dáil Éireann, 5 March 2015).

During her term as leader and Tánaiste her party played a major role in winding up Anglo Irish Bank, ending the bank guarantee and exiting the bailout. Burton's contribution was key to preventing the sell-off of State assets, protecting core welfare payments and increasing the minimum wage twice.

She was influential in removing 700,000 low-paid workers from the Universal Social Charge (USC) net, in placing collective bargaining on a statutory basis, and in ensuring that, through the Haddington Road and Lansdowne Road agreements, there would be no compulsory public sector redundancies. Thereby industrial peace was maintained and public services were protected.

In November 2014 she was trapped for hours in her ministerial car by protesters against water charges, and was eventually freed by Gardaí.

She piloted the Gender Recognition Act 2015, relating to transgender rights, through the Dáil. As Tánaiste she implemented a Labour commitment by achieving agreement on a referendum date on marriage equality for same sex couples. The *Yes* outcome of this referendum granting marriage equality was greeted with joy in Ireland and abroad, and was seen as evidence of modernisation.

In the 2016 general election, Labour was punished by the electorate for its role in implementing austerity measures in response to the financial crisis. The party returned to opposition.

*"I think that the right thing for that 2011 government to do was to turn the country around and get people back to work. I think it would be politically naive to expect that people would feel terribly grateful in the context of all the difficulties. But it was a national duty. The country needed to be rescued."*

(Burton, quoted in Hot Press. 11 April 2018).

In May 2016 Burton announced her resignation as Labour Party leader.

*"Politics is really interesting, fulfilling, a wonderful life. You get to work on ideas and issues that you're passionately interested in. I would strongly recommend it."* (Hot Press, 11 April 2018).

She resumed work on the back benches. She spoke with candour about her experiences as a child adopted through St. Patrick's Guild. She campaigned on adoption issues, and revealed problems she faced in tracing her birth parents. She sponsored the *Informal Adoptions (Regularisation) Bill 2019* which would allow those affected to make an application to the Circuit Court to register their legal adopted status.

*"Labour's best performer over the past five years".*
(Irish Independent 30 April 2007).

*"Was one of the stellar performers of the 29th Dáil."*
(Sunday Tribune, 20 May 2007).

*"Burton's grasp of the portfolio, her extraordinary work rate shadowing the finance minister and her vocal opposition to the state guarantee for Anglo Irish Bank proved a massive buttress for the Labour Party throughout 2010".*
(Sunday Business Post, 13 March 2011).

Joan Burton lost her seat in the general election of 8th February 2020.

Shortlisted for Campaigning Politician of the Year in the Magill Politician of the Year Awards 2005.

Winner, Magill Campaigning Politician of the Year 2007.

Shortlisted, Magill TD of the Year 2007.

Magill TD of the Year 2008.

# Frances Fitzgerald, née Ryan

Date/Place OF Birth: August 1950/Croom, County Limerick
PARTY: FINE GAEL
CONSTITUENCY:
DÁIL: DUBLIN SOUTH EAST/DUBLIN MID WEST;
SEANAD: LABOUR PANEL
DÁIL: 27TH-29TH (NOVEMBER 1992-JUNE 2002); 31ST (2011-2016); 32ND (26 FEBRUARY 2016-DATE)
SEANAD: 23RD (24 JULY 2007-25 JULY 2011)
AGE AT ENTRY TO DÁIL: 42
EUROPEAN PARLIAMENT: (MAY 2019 - )
FAMILY: MARRIED TO MICHAEL FITZGERALD, 3 SONS
EDUCATION: HOLY FAMILY SECONDARY SCHOOL, NEWBRIDGE, CO. KILDARE; SION HILL, BLACKROCK, CO.DUBLIN. UCD
(B. SOC. SC.). LONDON SCHOOL OF ECONOMICS (M.SC. IN SOCIAL ADMINISTRATION AND SOCIAL WORK)
Address: Georgian Village, Castleknock, Dublin 15

PUBLICATIONS: Fitzgerald, Frances, 'Women, Empowerment and Contemporary Ireland', in O'Connell, Maurice R., *People Power: Proceedings of the Third Annual Daniel O'Connell Workshop, Cahirciveen, Ireland,* Dublin: Institute of Public Administration on behalf of DOCAL — Daniel O'Connell Association, 1993. Co-author, with Gaffney, Conway and Andrews, of *Parenting: A Handbook for Parents.*

## Career:

Tánaiste, 6 May 2016 - 28 November 2017. Tánaiste and Minister for Business, Enterprise and Innovation, 14 Jun 2017-28 November 2017. Minister for Justice, 8 May 2014-14 June 2017.Minister for Children, March 2011-7 May 2014. Member, Joint Committee on the Constitutional Amendment on Children, 2007-2011; Joint Committee on Health and Children, 2007-2011; its sub-committee on Children. Member, Committee on Selection of Seanad Éireann, 2007-2011; Seanad Committee on Procedure and Privileges, 2007-11; Seanad Committee on Members' Interests, 2007-2011. Fine Gael Leader in Seanad Éireann, September 2007-. Fine Gael Seanad Spokesperson on Health and Children, October 2007-. Chair, National Women's Council. Vice-President, European Women's Lobby. Board Member, Arthritis Ireland; O'Reilly Theatre, Dublin. Europa Donna, Ireland (working for better cancer services).

Front-bench spokesperson on Defence, 1997. Front-bench spokesperson on Arts, Culture and the Gaeltacht, 1993-94. Member, Select Committee on Social Affairs, April 1993; Member, Joint Committee on Justice. Equality and Law Reform, 1997; of its Sub-Committee on Women's Rights,

1998. Chair, Council for the Status of Women, 1988-92. Member, Second Commission on the Status of Women, 1990-93. Vice President, Irish Council of the European Movement, 1991-3. Member, All-Party Constitutional Committee, 1997; Forum for Peace and Reconciliation, 1995-6, 1997. Board member of the Employment Equality Agency, 1987-91. Irish Representative to European Women's Lobby, 1988-92 (Vice-president, 1992). Chair, Women's Political Association 1987-9 (formerly Vice-chair and public relations officer). Board member, Dublin Institute of Adult Education, 1987-. Executive Committee member, Institute of European Affairs, 1993-.

**Frances Fitzgerald** was courted by several political parties before the 1992 election. As a high-profile Chair of the Council for the Status of Women, she was expected to attract a women's vote. Fianna Fáil appointed her to the Health Promotion Council. Shortly afterwards she agreed to run for Fine Gael.

She was elected first in 1992 as a FG TD for Dublin South-East, where she served until losing this seat in the 2002 Fine Gael electoral meltdown. She contested Dublin Mid-West in the general election of 2007, but was not elected. Elected to the Seanad in 2007 on the Labour panel, she was Opposition Leader in the Upper House until winning her Dáil seat in Dublin Mid-West in the 2011 election.

She was a member of a Fine Gael team which in 2001 proposed radical changes to the libel laws, offering greater freedom to journalists in return for better rights for aggrieved members of the public. She organised a successful national conference on breast cancer care in Dublin in May 2006.

Fitzgerald was an ally of party leader Enda Kenny, not least during the 2010 challenge to his leadership. In 2011 she was appointed the first Minster for Children of senior Cabinet rank, a portfolio which heretofore had been of junior ministerial status.

Her achievements in this ministry include the passage of the Children's Referendum, the Children First legislation and establishment of the Child and Family Agency, Tusla.

She piloted the referendum on children's rights - Thirty-First

Amendment of the Constitution Act (Children) 2012 - held in November 2012. As a result, an article was inserted in the Constitution, recognising that children have rights. Article 42A requires the State to legislate to permit adoption, including by voluntary placement, whether or not the parents are married, where the parents have failed in their duty, and where adoption is in the child's best interests.

In April 2012 she published the Heads of the Children First Bill. The actual *Children First Bill 2014*, published in April 2014, differed in many respects from the Heads of the Bill. The Children First Act was enacted in November 2015 to raise awareness of child abuse and neglect, provide for mandatory reporting by professionals, improve child protection and provide for inter-agency working. The Criminal Justice (Withholding of Information on Offences against Children and Vulnerable Persons) Act, 2012 and the National Vetting Bureau (Children and Vulnerable Persons) Act, 2012 complement the legislation designed to improve child safety and protection.

> *"She has succeeded in getting her department moving. She gave a superb response to the Cloyne Report into clerical child abuse where she showed a broad depth of knowledge and a hitherto unseen steel. She has been involved in updating child-protection guidelines."* (Irish Independent, 10 September, 2011).

Fitzgerald oversaw the structural change of moving 4,000 civil and public servants from the Health Service Executive into Tusla, the Child and Family Agency, which commenced in January 2014.

As Minister for Justice, she addressed concerns about corruption and other controversies in An Garda Siochána. She steered the Legal Services Bill through the Oireachtas against resistance and oversaw a state inquiry into miscarriages of justice.

In May 2014, she announced the government's intention to establish an independent board to appoint the next Garda Commissioner, following a succession of scandals in the police force.

In July 2014 she published the Report of the Independent Review Group on the Department of Justice and Equality, which recommended fundamental organisational and cultural renewal of the Department. She pressed on with reforms of the Gardaí and established a new oversight body, the Policing Authority.

Fitzgerald was re-appointed Minister for Justice when Taoiseach Kenny's second government was formed. More allegations of police malpractice were made. Fitzgerald sought through the Policing Authority answers from the force about its failures.

When on the first weekend of Leo Varadkar's party leadership campaign in 2017 she declared for Varadkar, her standing was such that "it was a sign that the contest was as good as over" (Irish Times,28 November 2017). In Taoiseach Varadkar's first Cabinet, Fitzgerald was retained as Tánaiste and moved from the Justice portfolio to Business, Enterprise and Innovation.

Fitzgerald was subjected to intense Opposition attacks about her handling of a Garda controversy involving allegations of a smear campaign against Garda Sgt. McCabe, who had made a disclosure of malpractice in the police force. She told Cabinet in November 2017 that she would be vindicated by the Disclosures Tribunal examining the allegations. On 28 November 2017, faced with a no-confidence Dáil motion on this issue which threatened to bring down the Government, the Tánaiste resigned from Government and returned to the back benches.

In 2018 she was vindicated by the interim Disclosures Tribunal reports. She was found to have acted appropriately and used her judgement well. She was said to have "selflessly" resigned from government in the national interest.

The Taoiseach praised her championing of women's and children's rights, and for fighting all forms of inequality and injustice.

*"She was one of the most reforming Ministers for Justice we have ever had. She always supported whistleblowers, and*

*enshrined a code of ethics in An Garda Síochána to protect them."*

She observed that women's achievements are not reported as often as men's and are not as visible. "We don't talk about the over-representation of men," she told a conference. She noted that politics is a tough business, with tremendous highs and terrible enough lows (Department of Justice and Equality. "Politics Needs Women" conference, Dublin, 14 December 2018).

In May 2019 she stood in the constituency of Dublin in the European elections and was elected to the European Parliament.

# Jan O'Sullivan, *née* Gale

Date/Place of Birth: 6 December 1950/Clonlara, County Clare
Party: Democratic Socialist Party, 1982-90; Labour, 1990 to date
Constituency: Limerick East (1997-2011); Limerick City (2011- )
Dáil/Seanad: 28th, 29TH, 30th, 31st, 32nd Dáil (12 March 1998 [by-election] - January 2020).
Seanad: 20th Seanad, Administrative Panel (1 February 1993-6 August 1997).
Age at Entry to Seanad: 42
Age at Entry to Dáil: 47
Family: Daughter of journalist (Limerick Echo and Leader).
Married to Dr.Paul O'Sullivan.
1 daughter. 1 son.
Education: St Michael's Primary School, Pery Square, Limerick. Villiers School, Limerick.
Trinity College Dublin (BA (Mod)); University College Cork (H.Dip.Ed.);
Montessori Dip. Ed.
Occupation: Secondary teacher; Montessori teacher
Address: Corbally, Limerick

## Career:

Minister for Education and Skills, 11 July 2014 - 6 May 2016. Minister of State at Department of the Environment, with responsibility for housing and planning, 20 December 2011-11 July 2014. Minister of State for Trade & Development at Department of Foreign Affairs & Trade, March - 20 December 2011. Member, Joint Committee on Children and Youth Affairs, 21 July 2016-. Member, Joint Committee on the Future Funding of Domestic Water Services, November 2016-. Member, Joint Committee on Health and Children, its Vice Chair, 2007-2011. Member, Committee on Article 35.4.1° of the Constitution and section 39 of the Courts of Justice Act 1924, 2004-. Vice-Chair, Joint Committee on Education and Science, 2002-. Member, Joint Committee on the Constitution, 2-31 July 2003 and All-Party Committee on the Constitution, 2002. Chair, All-Party Oireachtas Interest Group on Sexual and Reproductive Health and Rights and Development, European Parliamentary Forum on Population & Development (EPF).

Member, Joint Committee on Justice. Equality and Women's Rights, 1999-. Member, Limerick City Council 1985 -; Limerick VEC, 1985-91; Mid-western Health Board, 1991-; Mid-western Regional Authority, 1991-9; Mayor of Limerick, July 1993-4. Member, Forum for Peace and Reconciliation; Devolution Commission, 1996-7; Member, Board of Island Theatre Company, Limerick, Committee of Exhibition of Visual Arts. Chair, Limerick/ Quimper Twinning Committee. Director, Daghda Dance Company.

**Jan O'Sullivan** grew up in a village near Limerick.

*"As a child growing up Protestant in 1950s and 1960s Ireland, I was very conscious of being different. I lived in a small village in Clare and went to school in the city while all my neighbours went to the local primary school a minute's walk from our house. The Catholic church was beside the school and while I walked to church on Sundays with my parents and brother up the road, we met everyone else in the parish walking down the road to their church....I believe that being part of a minority group can make you resilient, self-reliant, questioning and understanding of others who are different in other ways."*

(Irish Times, 29 July 2019)

Having lived in Canada before returning to Ireland in the late 1970s, she entered politics because of her conviction that state intervention is needed to redress Imbalances in opportunities arising from circumstances of birth.

Her denominational background became an issue twice in 1993/1994 when, as Mayor of Limerick, she was prevented by Bishop Newman from reading a lesson at a Mass for Civic Week. She later shook hands with the bishop and made only a formal protest about the insult to the office of mayor. Similarly, she was prevented from speaking at the opening of a Christian Brothers school. Although both controversies arose simply from her non-Catholic status, she would not have endeared herself to the bishop in her role as one of 'Kemmy's Femmies' — the name given by opponents to those helping to run Limerick's first family-planning clinic in the 1970s.

Having become a councillor in 1985 for the Democratic Socialist Party, O'Sullivan followed its leader Jim Kemmy into Labour in 1990. She became Mayor of Limerick and a senator in 1993. From 1993 to 1997, she was Labour leader in the Seanad, where she was a member of the Forum for Peace and Reconciliation. Her pathbreaking was celebrated:

> 'Tis Jan, says he, of womanly charm
> Whisht now! let there be no alarm
> She has great intelligence and practical wit.
> And on the Seanad she does her bit.
> The battle raged and words clashed bitter.
> As robes of red 'neath bright lights glitter
> Jan, unperturbed, did stand and ponder
> This mighty Gale caused all to wonder

Extract from 'Welcome, Mayor Jan', by Maureen Sparling, from Ripples in the Sand, Limerick, Sparling, 1997, by kind permission of the poet.

As Kemmy's running mate in 1992, she came within a few hundred votes of taking a second Dáil seat, which established her as his successor when he died in 1998.

In the 1999 local elections, O'Sullivan became Limerick's first alderwoman (and its last, as the title was abolished by the Local Government Act 2001).

While opposition Labour spokeswoman on Equality and Law Reform, O'Sullivan attacked the government's handling of the asylum-seekers' issue, describing measures to combat abuse of immigration controls as an infringement of human rights. She introduced a Private Members Bill to extend the definition of a legal disability to victims of sexual or physical child abuse so they can take legal action even though the statutory limit has expired. This Bill was enacted as the *Statute of Limitations Amendment Act* 2000. Hundreds of victims of child abuse previously restricted from taking action could now do so, even though the government excluded physical abuse from the Bill. During 2004 she highlighted the extent of the special needs crisis in schools. (350 special needs teaching posts were subsequently created by the government). Her opposition role as education spokeswoman was noted.

> *"Hardly a day goes by without O'Sullivan sending a press release on education issues... The impressive thing is this: almost all are well researched and say something interesting".*

(Irish Times, 19 October 2004).

She contested the deputy leadership of the Labour Party in 2007 and polled well.

In her "super junior" ministerial position at Environment with responsibility for housing, O'Sullivan attended Cabinet, though without a vote. Her remit included homelessness, regeneration of blight, "ghost estates" of unfinished houses and householders in difficulty paying their mortgages. Her constituency clinics were located in some of Limerick's disadvantaged areas, Moyross, Southill and St Mary's Park. One of her key achievements as Minister of State for Housing was "to keep money flowing for the regeneration of these areas during the economic crisis". (Sunday Business Post, 12 April 2015).

O'Sullivan faced criticism for an increase in homelessness, low levels of social housing construction and the government's failure to end upward-only rent reviews.

As Minister for Education and Skills, O'Sullivan led trade missions to China and other countries to increase awareness of Irish higher education and to attract students. Legislation she sponsored included the Teaching Council Amendment Act 2015.

She continued the promotion of plurality in a church-dominated system by divesting schools of church patronage. She announced new multi-denominational schools under the patronage divesting process, while acknowledging that the pace of divesting was slow. She announced the abolition of Rule 68, which stated that religion is the most important aspect of primary school education.

O'Sullivan was among a handful of Labour TDs who retained their seats in the 2016 general election in which the Labour Party was punished by the electorate for its role in implementing austerity policies. She returned to the backbenches.

However, the Labour Party did not recover in the general election of 8th February 2020 and she lost her seat.

# Heather Humphreys, née Stewart

Date/Place of birth: 14 May 1963/Drum, Co. Monaghan
Party: Fine Gael
Constituency: Cavan-Monaghan
Dáil: 31st. (February 2011-February 2016);
32nd (26 February 2016-2020)
Age at entry to Dáil: 47
Family: Married to Eric Humphreys. 2 daughters.
Education: St Aidan's Comprehensive, Cootehill, Co Cavan.
Occupation: Manager of Cootehill Credit Union, Co Cavan;
former Ulster Bank official.
Address: Dernaroy, Newbliss, Co Monaghan.

**Career:**
Minister for Business, Enterprise and Innovation, 30 November 2017 - 2020.
Minister for Arts, Heritage and Culture, 14 June, 2017-30 November 2017.
Minister for Arts, Heritage, Regional, Rural and Gaeltacht Affairs, 6 May 2016 -
14 June 2017. Minister for Arts, Heritage and the Gaeltacht, 11 July, 2014 - 6
May 2016.

Member, Joint Oireachtas Committee on Finance; on Public Expenditure &
Reform; Joint Administration Committee, 2011-. Co-opted to Monaghan
County Council in 2003, elected to the Council in 2004, 2009. Mayor of County
Monaghan, 2009/2010.

Member, Organisation for Security and Co-Operation in Europe. Member,
National Commemoration Committee. Member of community groups, including
the campaign for the redevelopment of the Ulster Canal.

**Heather Humphreys** was raised as a Presbyterian in Drum in the border
county of Monaghan. Her father is a member of the Orange Order, while
her grandfather, Robert James Stewart, signed the Ulster Covenant
opposing Home Rule in 1912. ("My grandfather signed the Ulster
Covenant," Minister says. Irish Times, Jan 21, 2016).

*"To get to Drum in Co Monaghan – reckoned to be the Republic's only totally Protestant village – you have to go off the beaten track"* (Irish Times, Aug 8, 2016).


Having grown up on a farm and married a farmer, Humphreys is familiar with EU-funded farm payments under the Common Market policy. She brought her experience as a bank official and Credit Union manager to bear in her role as the Chair of Fine Gael's internal finance committee.

In the run-up to the *Protection of Life During Pregnancy Bill*, during a heated exchange with an anti-abortion TD at a Fine Gael party meeting, Humphreys was reported to have said that TDs and senators wanted the issue settled. She was cheered into the Members' bar afterwards by party colleagues (Irish Independent, 21 June 2013). Her support for this legislation addressing the consequences of the *X Case* court judgment elicited attacks from anti-abortion protesters. In July 2013 white crosses daubed in red paint were nailed onto telegraph poles near her Monaghan home.

An ally of Taoiseach Kenny, she received her first ministerial portfolio in the reshuffle of July 2014.

She told a newspaper that she enjoyed the *Yes, Minister* television series. The new minister arrived at her Department bearing her seal of office, and recounted her meeting with her Secretary General.

> *"He said, 'Congratulations Minister,' and I asked him to call me Heather. But he said 'No, this is the way we do things, we always use Minister'. And I said, 'Well if that's the way you do it, that's fine with me'. And he goes, 'Yes, Minister'. And I just thought 'here we go'"....*

(Irish Independent, 8 February 2015).


In the early months of Humphreys' ministerial career she had to defend a party decision to make an appointment to the board of the Irish

- 79 -

Museum of Modern Art. She became embroiled in controversy when a nominee was appointed to that board to boost his credentials in a Seanad by-election. As a result, a new system of recruiting members of state boards was inaugurated. Having weathered the storm, she had considerable success in the Arts department.

In 2016 as Minister of Rural Affairs, she de-designated some protected bogs, responding to bog-cutters and rural Independent TDs supporting the Government. The *Heritage Bill* extending the hedge-cutting season also alarmed bird conservation groups.

She was in charge of plans for the commemoration of the centenary of the 1916 Rising.

> *She performed really well during last year's 1916 commemorations, seamlessly accommodating her own Protestant background with what became an unabashed celebration of Irish nationalism and identity.*

(Irish Times, May 2, 2017)

In the 2017 budget she gained increases for the Arts Council, the National Library and the film industry. She introduced the Creative Ireland programme, to bring arts, culture, music, drama and software coding to every locality. In the same year she launched the Action Plan for Rural Development with 270 measures to address rural decline, including the funded Town and Village Renewal Scheme.

A major element of her role in the Department of Business, Enterprise and Innovation is addressing challenges to Ireland which could result from Britain leaving the European Union (Brexit), for which the UK electorate voted in 2016. Her Border county background was viewed as bringing valuable experience of Brexit-related issues.

> *Ms Humphreys is both talented and capable. She has proved herself to be a safe and loyal pair of hands.*

(Irish Independent, 1 December 2017).

In 2019 she was non-partisan in adopting opposition proposals on Bills relating to ticket-touting and gift vouchers. She declined to join politicians' angry reactions and beef farmers' opposition to the EU Mercosur trade deal with South American countries, because of the broader economic and trade implications which would benefit Ireland. She also took a strong line against insurance "compo culture" in a controversy involving a Fine Gael TD.

Her straight-talking and astuteness on these issues earned her the media accolade of Minister of the Year. (Irish Times, 20 July 2019).

# Mary Mitchell O' Connor

Date/Place of birth: 10 June 1959/
Milltown, Co. Galway
Party: Fine Gael
Constituency: Dún Laoghaire
Dáil: 31st (February 2011-2016); 32nd (2016 - 2020)
Age at entry to Dáil: 51
Family: Divorced. 2 sons.
Education: Presentation Convent, Tuam, Co Galway;
Carysfort College, Blackrock, Co Dublin. NUI Maynooth (Masters in Education and School Leadership). European Coaching Institute (Diploma in Life Coaching).
Occupation: Primary school principal
Address: Cabinteely, Co Dublin.

## Career:

Minister of State for Education with responsibility for higher education, 14 June 2017-2020. Minister for Jobs, Enterprise and Innovation, 6 May 2016-14 June 2017. Member, Joint Committee on Health and Children. Member, Joint Committee on Public Service Oversight and Petitions, 2012 - February 2016.Elected to Dún Laoghaire Rathdown County Council in 2004 as a Progressive Democrats councillor. Joined Fine Gael in 2007. Chair, Dún Laoghaire Area Committee for Transport, Economic Development and Planning, 2008-9. Re-elected to the County Council, 2009-2011. She contested the general election in 2011 and was elected in her first general election.

**Mary Mitchell O'Connor** was a school principal in Co. Meath and in The Harold School in Dublin. While a Councillor she resisted increases in commercial rates in an effort to keep business costs down, and campaigned against the re-introduction of university fees.

On her first day in parliament it was reported,

> '... nor was she too proud to say that this was a day she had yearned for. "I did a coaching course 2½ years ago and was visualising myself coming into Dáil Éireann." "So visualising stuff

*actually works?" squeaked an excited onlooker. "Well, I'm going to try and visualise myself now as a minister in five years' time,"* she said.

(Irish Times, 10 March 2011).

In January 2013 she expressed concerns about the equity of the new property tax based on a house's market value, saying that Dublin dwellers would be subsidising houses of equal and greater size and status in the rest of the country. She averred that the money collected in the capital would be spent in other counties (Daily Mirror, 14 January 2013), saying:

*"Many of the residents in these houses have the appearance of being asset rich but many are cash poor. This proposed tax does not take account of those who paid stamp duty of up to 9 per cent at the top end of the market. Many of those buyers had to borrow the money to pay that stamp duty. Many now are in negative equity or are in mortgage arrears."*

(Sunday Independent, 13 January 2013).

She held the Jobs portfolio during a recovering economy and continued the Action Plan for Jobs, with the result that over 66,000 jobs were created in 2016 and the unemployment rate continued to fall. She emphasised rural jobs and employment.

*When viewed against its very focused goal, the Action Plan for Jobs has to rank as one of the most successful policy programmes in the history of the state.*

(Sunday Business Post, 17 March 2019).

While Minister for Jobs, her proposal to give a lower tax rate to highly-skilled returning emigrants was not well received by the opposition or her party colleagues, although her predecessor had made the same suggestion 12 months before without being criticised.

She responded to the challenges caused by the 2016 British vote to leave the EU.

> *"She has done well on Brexit. She set up a Brexit unit in her department and boosted staffing in the IDA and Enterprise Ireland. She has played hardball with her British counterpart."*
>
> (Irish Times, May 2, 2017).

Mitchell O'Connor is an advocate of women's rights.

Having been subjected to sexist insults by male deputies in the Dáil Chamber, she defended colleagues similarly insulted.

> *Because we are a tiny minority within Dáil Eireann, I believe that every female deputy has a responsibility to constantly and relentlessly push back against disrespect and inappropriate behaviour, not just for ourselves, but for other women and for other minorities - and we do.*
>
> *However, we also have a function which must never be minimised, which is to provide role models for the next generation of women, to establish a reality which makes it appealing for women to become public representatives.*
>
> (Mary Mitchell O'Connor. 'We're supposed to craft laws, not shout personal insults'. Irish Independent, 17 July 2013).

While Minister for State at Education, the issue of how to fund higher education into the future was not addressed by her, according to the Irish Independent (13 July 2019).

She strove to improve the position of women academics. Though women constitute about half of university lecturers, they account for just under a quarter of professors and there had never been a female university president in 400 years of higher education.

She established a taskforce which proposed gender specific appointments to fund women-only professorships over the next three years to help "eradicate gender inequality" in higher education. These posts would be in addition to existing staff and confined to areas where there is "clear evidence" of significant under-representation of women, such as science or engineering.

She announced the implementation plan in November 2018. The plan was welcomed by women academics, who saw the scheme as a bold move with high impact which would "change the dynamic...in our understanding of women as research leaders" (NUIG University Women's Network, Irish Times, 19 July 2019). The initiative sparked controversy in some quarters over whether it flouted recruitment policies which promote equality of opportunity for men and women.

Her response was to tell a conference that the statistics proved that "academic posts are outrageously biased, in their distribution, towards men":

> "The bottom line is that for generations, men within academia have effectively confined hundreds of professorships and lectureships to men. Were any of those professorships or lectureships regarded as second rate as a result of that? Are you kidding? Yet the minute a female Minister says 'Lads, here's a handful of posts you can't go for. Here are a handful of posts that, by way of a tiny tilt towards equality, will be kept for women,' the view taken is negative."

> (Irish Independent, 7 March 2019).

However, the Attorney General confirmed that the initiative is consistent with EU and Irish employment and equality law (Irish Times, 22 June 2019).

Mitchell O'Connor in June 2019 opened applications to the "senior academic leadership initiative".

# Katherine Zappone

Date/Place of birth: 25 November 1953/Seattle, Washington state, USA.
Party: Independent
Constituency: Taoiseach's nominee (Seanad); Independent, Dublin South West (Dáil)
Seanad: $24^{th}$ ( 25 May 2011- 25 February 2016)
Dáil: $32^{nd}$ (26 February 2016 – January 2020)
Age at entry to Seanad: 57
Family: Married Ann Louise Gilligan
Education: Holy Names Academy, Seattle; Catholic University of America (MA), UCD (MBA), Boston College (PhD).
Occupation: Lecturer in Ethics, TCD. Director, Centre for Progressive Change.
Address: Glenaraneen, Brittas ,Co. Dublin.
Publications: Co-author of *Seanad Éireann: Open it, don't close it.* Radical Seanad reform through legislative change. Consultation Paper: Proposals for measures to transform Seanad Éireann without the need for constitutional amendment, September 2012. Zappone, Katherine. The hope for wholeness: a spirituality for feminists (1991); Re-thinking identity: the challenge of diversity (2003). Gilligan, Ann Louise and Katherine Zappone. Our lives out loud: in pursuit of justice and equality (2008).

## Career:
Minister for Children and Youth Affairs, 14 June 2017-2020. Member, Seanad Public Consultation Committee, 2011-2016. Member, Parliamentary Assembly of the Council of Europe (2012-2013); Member, Rapporteur PACE Committee on equality and Non-Discrimination. Member, Joint Committee on Justice, Defence and Equality. Member, Irish Human Rights Commission (2000-2011). CEO, National Women's Council of Ireland (1997-2000).

**Katherine Zappone** grew up in the United States and became an Irish citizen in 1995. She is the first openly lesbian member of the Oireachtas and also the first in a same-sex marriage.

In 1981, while studying at Boston College, Zappone met Ann Louise Gilligan, with whom she celebrated a life-partnership ceremony in 1982. They moved to Ireland in 1983. A decade after first meeting the couple were married in Canada. The couple founded An Cosán (The Path), a centre of second-chance education for women in disadvantaged Dublin areas. An Cosán grew into Ireland's largest community education organisation supporting over 1,000 families annually, and runs an early childhood facility, Rainbow House, and Fledglings social enterprise, which operates eight community pre-schools.

Senator Lynn Ruane credits Gilligan and Zappone's visionary and altruistic work in education by founding An Cosán as having a profound impact on her life.

(Irish Times, 19 June 2017).


Zappone came to prominence when she and Gilligan sought legal recognition in Ireland for their Canadian marriage. The Revenue Commissioners turned down their application to be taxed as a married couple. The couple took a landmark High Court case: *Zappone and Gilligan v Commissioners of Inland Revenue, Ireland and the Attorney General 2006.* Ivana Bacik was one of their lawyers. The High Court declined to recognise their Canadian marriage. Zappone and Gilligan opened fresh legal proceedings, arguing (on slightly revised grounds) that, far from precluding same-sex marriage, the Constitution precludes a ban on it.

Their quest for legal change and their campaigning culminated first in the Civil Partnership Act of 2010 and then the success of the marriage-equality referendum of 22 May 2015.

Besides the massive contribution Gilligan made to education, she and Katherine Zappone were the spark that lit the marriage equality movement in Ireland, a spark that continues to light the way for broader social change. By taking a case to have their Canadian marriage recognised in Ireland, they inspired a movement. They lost in the High Court, but the genie was out of the bottle. The idea of marriage rights existing for same-sex couples in Ireland could not be undreamed. In the LGBT community, Gilligan and Zappone became a shorthand: KAL. The organisational support that formed around their case became the KAL Advocacy Initiative, and in turn that became Marriage Equality, which was the organisational driver of advocating for marriage rights for LGBT people. Marriage Equality also became an integral part of Yes Equality which organised, fought, and won the marriage referendum campaign. The structures that were put in place, that evolved as the movement took hold, and that led to the referendum win, originated with Gilligan and Zappone and those who organised around them.

(Irish Times, 19 June 2017).


On 23 May 2015, Zappone asked her wife Ann Louise Gilligan live on air to re-marry her in Ireland now that it had voted "Yes" to marriage equality.

Zappone was a leader of the successful campaign to retain the bicameral parliamentary system in Ireland when abolition of the Seanad was proposed by referendum in 2013. She co-sponsored the Seanad Bill 2013, proposing to give every citizen a vote in Seanad elections, gender equality in a reformed Seanad, and to extend the franchise to emigrants and Northern Ireland. Although the Bill lapsed on the dissolution of parliament, it was influential in the debate.

In 2014 Zappone served as grand marshal of the Seattle St. Patrick's Day parade.

She was elected to the Dáil as an Independent TD in 2016. Zappone made the Citizens' Assembly a condition of her joining the minority government---she told the Sunday Business Post in January 2017 that she would walk out of government if it did not act on the Assembly recommendations. (Sunday Business Post, 27 May 2018). The Citizens'

Assembly voted in favour of the Eighth Amendment ban on abortion being removed from the Constitution. This paved the way for the referendum on this issue in May 2018, which decided by a two to one majority to remove the Eighth Amendment from the Constitution. Zappone was the first member of cabinet to speak out in favour of repeal of the Eighth Amendment. As an Independent member of Cabinet, she was critical to securing support of Cabinet colleagues for the holding of a referendum and advocating for a 'Yes' vote to enable legalisation of abortion in Ireland (2017-18).

Minister Zappone established in 2016 the Working Group on Reforms and Supports for the Childminding Sector in 2016. Childminders caring for children in the childminder's home had been largely unfunded, unsupported and unregulated by the state. The Working Group submitted recommendations in March 2018. In August 2019 she launched for public consultation the Draft Childminding Action Plan, proposing to extend supports and regulation to all paid, non-relative childminders.

Zappone piloted through the Houses the Childcare Support Bill 2017, the "first ever legislation on childcare support for families", and fought for extra funding for childcare. When the Adoption (Information and Tracing) Bill proved controversial she paused it in order to listen to the stakeholders' concerns.

She addressed systems failures at Tusla which had led to mishandling of child sex abuse allegations. She showed compassion in dealing with delicate issues such as illegal birth registrations, and issues relating to mother-and-baby homes. Mother-and-baby homes were generally run by nuns for women pregnant outside marriage. (In the main their babies were adopted. Many were adopted by Catholic families in the US in return for a donation.) Zappone's proposal for a phased, forensic excavation of the infant burials at the Tuam mother-and-baby home was approved at Cabinet in October 2018.

She visited New York, Oxford and Belfast to see centres where police and social workers work in the same office with a view to enabling this arrangement in Ireland.

In February 2019 Zappone announced a 50 per cent increase in Ireland's annual contribution to the Global Fund, for the eradication of Aids, TB and malaria epidemics around the world. She thereby stood up for Ireland's record against Bill Gates' assertion that there were countries that could provide more funding to combat these diseases whose commitments had "plateaued". (Irish Times, 16 February 2019).

She lost her seat in the general election of 8th February 2020 and announced her retirement from politics.

Tatler Woman of the Year, 2016.

GALA Politician of the Year, 2017.

# Regina Doherty, née Dalton

Date/Place of birth: 26 January 1971/Dublin
Party: Fine Gael
Constituency: Meath East
Dáil: 31st. (February 2011-2016); 32nd (2016-2020)
Age at entry to Dáil: 40
Family: Married to Declan Doherty.
2 daughters. 2 sons.
Education: St Mary Holy Faith, Glasnevin.
College of Marketing and Design, Mountjoy Square, Dublin.
Occupation: Sales; Company director in IT sector
Address: Ratoath, Co Meath.

**Career:**
Minister for Employment Affairs and Social Protection, 14 June 2017 - 2020. Government Chief Whip and Minister of State at the Department of the Taoiseach, 6 May 2016 - 14 June 2017. Member, Business Committee, 9 June 2016-; Committee on Procedure (Dáil), 16 June 2016-; Sub-Committee on Dáil Reform, 16 June 2016-. Member, Joint Committee on Health and Children; Joint Committee on Finance; Public Expenditure and Reform; Joint Committee on the implementation of the Good Friday Agreement. Member, Constitutional Convention.
Contested the 2007 general election. Member, Meath County Council, 2009-2011. Chair, Meath's Joint Policing Committee. Board member, Meath VEC, Ratoath College and Gaelscoil na Mí. Member, Special Education Committee of the National Parents' Council.

**Regina Doherty** was politicized as a child:

*"I grew up being Fine Gael. Mam and Dad have always been very political. They are normal, working-class people, and my dad worked as a driver in the ESB when they got married. They didn't have their own house, so they lived with my Auntie Bess. After I was born, they got their first house, which was a council*

*house, in Ballymun - years later, we moved to Finglas. Mam and Dad were so grateful to this Fine Gael councillor who helped them, that they asked what they could do for her. She told them that they could set up a branch of Fine Gael in Ballymun, and they did...*

*Everything in our house revolved around Fine Gael, and there was a huge sense of solidarity within our branch. I remember the joys of leaflet-dropping and election campaigns. As a child, I actually thought that we were related to Garret FitzGerald [party leader/ Taoiseach] because we spent so much time following him through fields and on election trails. I was brought everywhere. I made my Communion on the same day as the Fine Gael Ard Fheis, so I was at that in my frock. I made a fortune.*

*All of this sparked an interest in politics, which a lot of my friends didn't share. I'd go into school talking about what happened on Today Tonight, while everyone else would have watched Knots Landing."*

(*Waking hours with Fine Gael TD Regina Doherty.* Irish Independent, February 23 2015).

Known as a good communicator, Doherty had challenges during her early years as a TD (Irish Times, 15 June, 2017). These included financial issues relating to the company she ran with her husband, her tense relationship with FG constituency colleague and minister of state Helen McEntee, and her performance as Whip.

"She has modified her social views in recent years and is a strong 'ideas' person." (ibid.)

Doherty revealed the intimidation faced by TDs who supported government legislation, the Protection of Life during Pregnancy Bill 2013. The purpose of this Bill, introduced as a result of the *X Case* court judgment, was to legalise abortion where there is a substantial risk to the mother's life, including the risk of suicide. She contacted Gardaí after anti-abortion activists threatened to harm her and her children and to burn down her house. Doherty believed that she was subjected to vitriol because of her decision to support this government Bill notwithstanding her conservative views.

Doherty was supportive of women entering politics:

> *"We don't sell the idea of a political career to mothers. Many stay-at-home moms could do what I did and be a successful local councillor earning €16,000 but they think it's not possible — it is and I wish we could get that message across."*

> (Irish Independent, 8 April 2013).

As Fine Gael's Deputy Director of Elections for the Seanad abolition referendum in 2013, she drew fire from senators reacting to a FG press release. One Senator used egregious terms. (Seanad Order of Business, 15 July 2013). On foot of an official complaint by Doherty, this Senator withdrew his remarks, regretting "any offence". Her colleague Mary Mitchell O'Connor (qv) on radio branded the remarks 'sexist and crude'.

Doherty discovered how backbenchers could influence policy:

> *"I never realised just how much you could influence policy decision as a lowly backbencher, but if you've got a big mouth and you push, you can."*

> (*Waking hours with Fine Gael TD Regina Doherty.* Irish Independent, 23 February 2015).

Heretofore an outspoken critic of Sinn Féin, she broke ranks in January 2017 by suggesting that she would be open to entering coalition with that party.

As Minister, Doherty in January 2018 launched the consultation to expand the Gender Recognition Act 2015 to include under-18s and non-binary people.

She initiated reforms to the pension system and confirmed the Government's intention to introduce pension auto-enrolment from 2022. The idea is to have all private sector workers over a certain age and income automatically sign up for a pension to which the employee, employer and State contribute. From 2020, the Government will reform the State contributory pension so that entitlement is based on the total number of PRSI contributions made over a person's working life.

Plans were announced in 2019 for extended parental leave, including another two weeks for fathers. As figures showed that already around 60% of men do not avail of existing paternity leave, Doherty referred to men not taking up the options. Her suggestion that the low uptake of paternity leave was because of a lack of interest from new fathers met with criticism. She responded that there's still a perception "in much public discussion that caring is a 'woman's thing' and that taking time off 'real work' is still a novelty for fathers" (Irish Independent, 25 April, 2019).

Doherty lost her seat in the general election of 8th February 2020.

# Josepha Madigan

Date/Place of birth: 21 May 1970/Dublin
Party: Fine Gael
Constituency: Dublin Rathdown
Dáil: 32$^{nd}$ (28 February 2016- )
Age at entry to Dáil: 45
Family: Married to Finbarr Hayes. 2 sons.
Daughter of Cllr. Paddy Madigan (Fianna Fáil/ later
Independent member of Dublin County Council and
Dún Laoghaire Corporation, 1980s - 1990s).

Education: Convent of the Sacred Heart, Mount Anville; Trinity College Dublin;
Law Society, Dublin.
Occupation: Solicitor.
Address: Mount Merrion, Co. Dublin.
Publications: *Appropriate dispute resolution (ADR) in Ireland.* Jordan Publishing,
2012; *Negligent behaviour* (a novel), 2011. "We need to speak freely in the
Dáil," by Josepha Madigan (Sunday Times, 18 December 2016).

## Career:

Minister for Culture, Heritage and the Gaeltacht, 30 November, 2017-. Chair,
Committee on Budgetary Oversight (July 2016 - November 2017). Member,
Committee of Public Accounts (16 June 2016-c.July 2017); Joint Committee on
Children and Youth Affairs (21 July 2016-); Committee on the Future of
Healthcare (01 June 2016-); Committee on Procedure (Dáil)

(16 June 2016- ). Member, Dun Laoghaire-Rathdown County Council, May 2014
until 2016-her election as a T.D. Mediator, certified by the Mediators' Institute
of Ireland (MII). MII Council member, specialist liaison officer for family
mediation with the Institute. Family Lawyer of the Year 2014, Irish Law Awards.

**Josepha Madigan** entered elected office as a local councillor in 2014.
She was elected to the Dáil in the general election of 2016, and

participated in government formation talks. By 2017 she had been appointed a Cabinet minister.

Her constituency of Dublin Rathdown had once been Constance Markievicz's (qv) constituency of Dublin St. Patrick's.

Madigan grew up in a political household. Her father, Councillor Paddy Madigan, had in 1981 succeeded in his challenge to the constitutionality of the Rent Restrictions Act, thereby freeing landlords significantly from the constraints of rent control. He also opposed residential property tax (Irish Times, April 26, 2014).

In 2017 she suggested that homeowners in her constituency would be hit disproportionately by local property tax [LPT] once new valuations would commence in November 2019. She urged that LPT calculations be based on site value or the size of a property rather than the market value.

> "Both have the benefit of relative price stability and would spread the LPT burden more evenly across the country," she said, adding that giving local authorities greater power to amend local rates could also assist in addressing this problem.

> (Irish Times, 31 July 2017)

She campaigned for victims to be exempted automatically from legal aid fees in domestic violence cases, pointing to 16,000 reported incidents of domestic abuse recorded in Ireland in 2015 alone (The Times (Ireland),1 August 2017).

In her first year in the Dáil Madigan was a prolific author of private members' legislation. She aimed to cut the waiting time for a divorce from four years to two, by tabling a private member's bill, the Thirty-Fifth Amendment of the Constitution (Divorce) Bill 2016. She pointed out that this measure would help up to 250,000 people who are separated (Sunday Times, 4 December 2016). Her proposals were accepted by Government. The electorate voted in favour of this measure in the referendum of May 2019.

Her work-rate was noted by the media.

> Busiest newcomer: (aka, the 'don't let the grass grow under your feet' award): Jointly to Josepha Madigan and Kate O'Connell. Madigan has already brought forward a private member's bill to reduce the period of separation necessary to obtain a divorce — surely some kind of record for a new TD.
>
> (Sunday Independent, 24 July 2016).

In July 2017 she announced that she would prepare a private member's bill to curb social media comments by strengthening rules on commentary about criminal trials.

> *"We cannot know how much such commentary is seen by jurors and what effect it might have. But we must protect the independent reputation of all juries"*
>
> (Irish Independent, 3 July 2017).

This Contempt of Court Bill to codify contempt of court laws was also accepted by government.

She called for a referendum to remove from the Constitution its Article 41.2.1, which provides that the state "shall endeavour to ensure mothers shall not be obliged by economic necessity to engage in labour to the neglect of her duties in the home". (Sunday Times, 23 July 2017). Research showed that opinion on this issue was divided and the matter was referred to a Joint Committee of the Oireachtas.

She defended the concept of Dáil privilege and the Committee on Procedure and Privilege safeguards to prevent abuses. ("We need to speak freely in the Dail," By Josepha Madigan, Sunday Times, 18 December 2016).

Madigan was appointed Minister for Culture, Heritage and Gaeltacht in a reshuffle caused by the resignation of Frances Fitzgerald (qv). She is Ireland's first gender-quota Dáil election candidate to be appointed to Cabinet.

In her first ministerial TV appearance she responded to news that there would be no prosecutions of Gardaí who had cancelled thousands of penalty points and fines by calling for those Gardaí to be disciplined.

The Taoiseach appointed her to a new cabinet sub-committee on the issue of justice and equality where she would drive the agenda on gender equality (Nomination of Government: Motion. 30 November 2017).

Madigan was Fine Gael campaign co-ordinator of the Yes campaign to repeal the Eighth Amendment of the Constitution in May 2018. The electorate voted *Yes* to repeal this ban on abortion.

In June 2018 she was rostered to read the lesson at Mass in her local church. Upon the non-arrival of the officiating priest, she addressed the congregation and led prayers (Irish Independent, 25 June 2018). For this she was rebuked by the Catholic Archbishop of Dublin. She responded: "The only agenda I am pushing is one of equality. I feel there should be equality in the church just as I believe there should be equality in all facets of society"(RTÉ, 27 June 2018).

In her capacity of Minister for Culture, Heritage and the Gaeltacht, she spearheaded the Government's programme to commemorate the centenary of women's suffrage in 2018.

Minister Madigan performed her own poem, *Diet Coke*, at a Culture Night poetry event in the Seanad Chamber to mark the 100th anniversary of women's suffrage

(Irish Times 22 September, 2018).

# Further Reading

Fitzgerald, Martina. Madam politician: the women at the table of Irish political power. Dublin, Gill, 2018.

McNamara, Maedhbh and Paschal Mooney. Women in parliament: Ireland 1918-2000. Dublin, Wolfhound, 2000.

McNamara, Maedhbh. Women in parliament 1918-2000 with directory of Women in Dáil, Seanad and Presidency 1918-2018. Sea Dog Books, forthcoming.

White, Anthony. Irish parliamentarians: deputies and senators 1918-2018. Dublin, Institute of Public Administration, 2018.

# Women government ministers 1919-2019

Constance Markievicz

Máire Geoghegan-Quinn

Eileen Desmond

Gemma Hussey

Mary O'Rourke

Niamh Bhreathnach

Nora Owen

Mary Harney

Síle de Valera

Mary Coughlan

Mary Hanafin

Joan Burton

Frances Fitzgerald

Jan O'Sullivan

Heather Humphreys

Mary Mitchell O'Connor

Katherine Zappone

Regina Doherty

Josepha Madigan

# Acknowledgments

I express my deep gratitude to those who helped me in the preparation of this book.

To Joan Burton TD for her inspiration and her foreword.

To those who were generous with advice and knowledge: Johanna Lowry O'Reilly, Dr. Sinéad McCoole, Gillian Kelly, Dr. Fiona Buckley, Dr. Claire McGing, Professor Yvonne Galligan, Dr. Patrick Melvin, Séamus Haughey, Aisling Maguire, Miriam Smith, Lorraine West, Dave O'Donoghue and Deirdre Devine and Michelle Bradley of Choice Publishing.

To those whose encouragement and amiability heartened me: Alexandra and Joe Roxborough, Aengus Byrne and Caitríona O'Malley, Sandra and Kenneth Foy, McNamara family, Oireachtas colleagues, Carmel Lambert and Gerard MacMichael, Mary and Michael Russell, Noreen Walshe and Gerry Harte, Anne and Tommy Griffin, Catherine Kelly, Micheál ÓCinnéide and Ann Hope, Maggie and Shay Garvey, Mary and Frank Gilmartin, Albert and Helen Conlon.

My greatest debt is to Seán Byrne, for his stellar support.

## About the author

Maedhbh McNamara grew up in counties Kerry, Galway, Louth and Limerick. She has been a research officer in the European Pilot Programme to Combat Poverty and the Oireachtas Library and Research Service.